THE *Spirit* OF LO

Gertrude,

   We hope all is
well with you
and your family.
      Your friends,
      Kerry

      Don

THE Spirit OF LO

An Ordinary Family's Extraordinary Journey

TERRY & DON DETRICH

MIND MATTERS, INC.
TULSA, OKLAHOMA

For information, please contact Mind Matters, Inc., P.O. Box 52503, Tulsa, Oklahoma 74152-0503.

First printing 2000.
Printed and bound in the United States of America.
Cover Illustration by Amanda Ramsey.
Book Design by Susan Coman, Protype, Inc.

Detrich, Terry
    The spirit of Lo: an ordinary family's extraordinary journey / Terry Detrich, Don Detrich. -- 1st ed.
    p. cm.
    ISBN: 0-9701934-0-8

    1. Cystic fibrosis—Patients. 2. Dietrich family. 3. Family.
I. Detrich, Don. II. Title

    RC858.C95D48 2000   616.37'00922
                          QBI00-500127

LCCN: 00-191552

To order contact (see order form on back page):
MIND MATTERS, INC.
P.O. Box 52503
Tulsa, Oklahoma 74152-0503
Tollfree: 1-877-222-2095
e-mail: www.SpiritofLo.com

Quantity discounts available on bulk purchases.
For information, please contact Mind Matters, Inc.

To our parents who taught us how to be
and
to our friends who continue
to wage the war against cystic fibrosis.

ACKNOWLEDGEMENTS

Our efforts to write this book over the last five years would never have been successful but for the help of many others. First and foremost, we thank our daughters, Jane and Lo, for their love, cooperation, and understanding. Second, we thank Sally Dennison for her editing skills and insights and Susan Coman for her design expertise. Third, we thank those who encouraged us to write a book in the first place and helped us believe that the completion of the project was worthwhile, continually offering their suggestions as the pages were written and rewritten — time and again: Bill Thomas, Elizabeth Beeton, Sue Gerkin, Pam Carter, Mary and Frank Dunn, Alma Robson, Phil Burns, Kathy and Markus Hilti, Julie and Phil Allen, Gretchen Thomas, Cathey Cravens and so many other friends and family members whose reviews provided direction and inspiration.

TABLE OF CONTENTS

Chapter I

DEADLY DIAGNOSIS

It was an Indian summer morning in October of 1984. My wife, Terry, and I sat stiffly in plastic-backed metal chairs in a suffocatingly little examination room. Terry held our three-month old infant daughter, Lauren, who slept peacefully, oblivious to the purpose that had brought us to this place. I searched for something upon which to focus, something that could distract me from thoughts of the anguish I felt.

A single window framed a view of the building's interior courtyard. Some courtyard. Silver pipes, stained by decades of rust, clutched dirty orange brick walls. Here and there, a brave strand of ivy sought to adorn the man-made blight. My gaze shifted to my wife. Her green eyes, normally full of sparkle, looked tired and sad as they stared blankly out the window. Her long blonde hair was pulled back, away from her face. She looked fatigued, I thought. I reached over and squeezed her shoulder. Our eyes met, but as if their encounter would demand more control than we had, it was for only an instant.

Endless minutes passed, one silent thought echoing another, as we waited for the news we both anticipated and dreaded. We could hear the doctor's voice through the wall, talking on the phone. We could hear him hang up and push his chair back. A moment of silence preceded the sound of his footsteps — out of his office and down the hallway to our room. A rustle of papers finally signaled the wait was over. He knocked on the door. Terry grabbed my hand, still resting on her shoulder. The doctor walked in. It was an Indian summer morning when we were told our baby girl had a deadly disease.

"Cystic fibrosis is the worst diagnosis I have to make." Doctor Kramer, a complete stranger to us, yet a man upon whom we were going to be totally dependent, delivered the first blow. He smiled faintly, nodded, and briefly closed his eyes as the venomous words sank in. I glanced at my tiny daughter sleeping in her mother's arms. Already, the tears were spilling down Terry's cheeks, one by one dropping onto the pastel cloud wrapped gently around our infant.

Every muscle in my body drew tight, my fists clenched instinctively. I wanted to hit that doctor but I couldn't. I could only sit there as he predicted each cruel symptom my child would endure. "There's no easy way to put this. The disease gradually chokes and starves its victims to death. Congestion throughout the respiratory system provides a breeding ground for bacterial infections, constricting the airways and destroying the lungs. Enzymes are blocked in the pancreas, preventing the patient's ability to absorb food."

I recalled how Terry had nursed our daughter day and night for the past three months. Lauren had still failed to gain weight. She had ravenously fed at her mother's breast, in addition to sucking down bottle after bottle of formula, only to lose the nutrients her body immediately dismissed as waste. I thought about the barely audible cough we had commented was odd coming from a baby. An insidious enemy had been attacking my little girl from within, Dr. Kramer was telling us. Its assault had begun at the hour of her conception.

"This disease is genetic," he looked each of us squarely in the eye. "Neither one of you did anything to cause your child to have it. Sometimes parents feel inordinately guilty." He paused again, shifting his eyes from Terry, to me, and then to our baby. "It's not your fault," he repeated. We had read this was true. His words offered a vague absolution, but didn't change our predicament.

He proceeded to describe a litany of grim statistics, one after another as if to get them all out on the table at once. "Cystic fibrosis kills more children than any other genetic illness," he said. "Right now, the life expectancy is twenty years. Each one of those years takes a heavy toll on the patient and family. Patients typically spend several weeks a year in the hospital. The incidence of divorce among parents is extremely high. Siblings often feel neglected and need professional counseling. If they live long enough, patients usually run out of insurance, leaving the burden of cost on the family. There are also substantial expenses that aren't covered."

I looked at this bespectacled man whose words were so completely obliterating our happy existence. He had been recommended to us as an esteemed specialist in cystic fibrosis. He was sixty-ish, rather slightly built, clad in gray pants, a lime green uniform shirt, bolo tie and cowboy boots. He didn't appear to be the kind of man who would enjoy decimating anyone's life. But he had yet to pull a single punch. He was all business.

Next, he asked us a series of questions, taking copious notes as we answered. Occasionally he would look up at whoever was speaking but most of the time he just wrote. When had we first noticed our daughter's failure to thrive? How much did she eat? How many diapers did we change each day? How often did she cough? Did we know of any relatives in our ancestry who had died at childbirth or shortly after? "The medical community still has very little understanding of the disease," he explained as if defending his inquisition. "It has mystified us for decades. Each case is unique."

He continued writing for a long time, leaving Terry and me to our pain. Terry's tears had ceased, her eyes looked empty, lost, sad. I could feel the sweat dripping down my brow, a steady throbbing at my temples. I looked around the examination room, this place that would forever entomb the vestiges of our naiveté. We had come hoping for assurances of our child's healthy development and instead received a sentence of death.

"So, Doctor, that's the best news you could give us?" I finally offered as I noticed him closing the file. My feeble attempt at humor was returned with a passing smile. This was not an easy meeting for him, either. How do you tell a couple of kids — for that's what we were at the time — that their lives are going to be changed and challenged in ways they could never have dreamed? How do you soften the blow that a family, and particularly a new baby, is not going to live happily ever after?

"Is there anything at all we can do?" Terry summoned the courage to ask. Her question, I knew, was as much a plea as anything.

"Ah — yes. I'm just getting to that," Dr. Kramer nodded and put his pencil down. Slowly, almost methodically, he folded his hands, closed his eyes as he had done before and positioned the heel of his boot on the bottom rung of the metal stool. It was as if he was situating himself physically while locating a particular place in his mind, a vantage point reserved for delivering a speech he'd given too often. Finally, he opened his eyes and took a deep breath. "The care of a cystic fibrosis patient is demanding," his lecture began. "It takes time and energy. But we believe the aggressive treatment of symptoms will keep our patients healthier and allow them to survive longer."

"We'll do whatever it takes." I said.

"Of course," Dr. Kramer acknowledged, then continued. "She'll need supplemental enzymes to digest fats. I recommend a special formula that has been pre-digested. It should help her begin to gain weight."

"Does that mean I have to stop nursing her?" Terry interrupted.

Dr. Kramer looked at her before answering straightforwardly. "We believe the pre-digested formula provides the best form of nutrition for patients."

"Oh."

Our infant was skin and bones, too weak to hold up her head anymore. But I knew from the expression on Terry's face that this was a blow of another kind. Breastfeeding had been a small gift, a means by which Terry had felt she'd helped keep Lauren alive. Now, even this small maternal comfort was going to be snatched away because of cystic fibrosis.

"I'll prescribe vitamins and minerals to help replace some of the other nutrients she can't absorb," Dr. Kramer's lecture droned on for several more minutes. Though we hung on every word, so as not to miss important instructions that might affect our child, the message was bleak. "As she gets sicker, we'll add more medications. In a few months, you'll need to start physical therapy." Dr. Kramer finally picked up his pencil again and made some check marks on a piece of paper. "That's about it for now," he smiled politely. "I'd like to examine your daughter in two weeks." He shook our hands on his way out, leaving the door open for the nurse who entered and presented us with a stack of brochures and prescriptions. We left the office in a state of shock; our child's deadly diagnosis had become a reality.

Chapter 2

GOING HOME

On the three-mile drive home inconsolable silence reflected the burden of my thoughts. The baby still slept. Don, my husband, drove, his eyes fixed on the road ahead. The world around me looked oddly strange, though this was Tulsa, the town in which I had lived my entire life. I knew the streets, every bump and curve. I knew the houses, the yards, the trees and flowers. I could still picture children in those homes, kids with whom I had grown up, riding bicycles, driving cars, sharing secrets and slumber parties. We had laughed and cried our way through elementary and high school, accumulating the knowledge that comes with friendships built upon so many lessons of adolescence. Experience had taught me to trust my world. It had been solid and sure. Till today.

Or, I pondered, perhaps my little universe had begun crumbling three months ago when I bore this infant girl. Her birth, in every way, had been an anomaly. I knew this was true because I'd already had one child. Jane, now three and a half years old, *had come out of the womb smiling through her screams, lunging headfirst into the challenges of life. Eager to nurse, ready to play, Jane was thirsty for experience. Her development raced along, physically and mentally. Don and I embraced parenting our first-born with joy.*

But even in delivery, I sensed things would be different with our second child. Crisis foreshadowed what was yet to come, as a cascade of obstacles threatened Lauren's emergence into humanity. The anesthetic I was given caused my blood pressure to plummet, diverting the doctors' attention away from her, though she was already in a state of distress. Then, seconds after birth, Don and I were forced to watch through a wall of glass as a team of peri-natal specialists stuck imposing tubes down our newborn's diminutive throat to vacuum out meconium waste that had infiltrated her lungs. In the midst of this procedure, we were moved into a recovery room, left to worry and wonder, to pray and wait for news of our infant.

In the meantime, I went through the motions of afterbirth, of post labor pains and sweats, of bleeding and chills. I was aware that my body was performing exactly as it should, but my mind and heart were in a state of shock, desperate to see and hold this life that had been part of my own for the last nine months.

I lay on the bed cart, holding Don's hand. It was as cold as mine, but strong and comforting at the same time. We said very little, separately trying to deal with all the "what ifs" the situation brought to mind. The exhilaration of childbirth was replaced with the terror of complications. Finally, after enduring an interminable wait, which may truly have only spanned an hour or two, a nurse opened the door of our room. "She's been taken to the nursery. She's going to be okay."

Shortly thereafter, Lauren Chevalier Detrich was ushered into our waiting arms, where we scrutinized her for ourselves, and eventually concurred that she was in fact, normal, and in truth, a beautiful baby girl. Our elation and relief was short-lived, however, as she lost an abnormal amount of weight over the next three days. The pediatrician tried to assure us that it was due to the difficult labor, but the pallor of our infant's complexion, almost translucent, blended with the fresh memories of delivery complications, left a foreboding sense that our troubles were not over.

A week later, at her first examination, she had dropped yet another half a pound. Again, the doctor insisted there was nothing to worry about. Still, I determined I would help my baby turn the tide by her next check-up. I nursed her every other hour. She ate eagerly but within seconds after starting to feed, her bowels would move. It was almost like she had chronic diarrhea, but since she didn't appear to be in discomfort, I decided to hope that time would take care of the problem. Maybe her digestive system needed to mature a bit. I knew my milk had been sufficient for one child. Surely, I reassured myself, if I just feed this new baby often enough, she'll retain adequate nutrition to begin to grow.

My efforts received a reward the next week as Lauren's weight stabilized. We breathed another momentary sigh of relief. In the days to come, however, she remained gaunt and pale. She gained an ounce here and there but I knew the effort it was taking to feed her far surpassed what it should have required.

During the perpetual nursing sessions, I was comforted by Lauren's presence. Though fragile, she seemed to have a kind of beauty that fostered serenity. Her blue eyes reflected a gentle countenance that calmed my nerves, frazzled as they became over her first months of life. Still, I found myself torn by worry and frustration.

"This is ridiculous," I complained to Don one evening after we put the girls to bed. "I can't tell the days from the nights." At the pediatrician's suggestion, we had started supplementing with bottles but continued feeding Lauren around the clock. My body ached, clamoring for restorative sleep. "I can't go on like this forever." I collapsed onto the couch, leaning my head wearily back onto the pillow cushion.

Don turned off the television and moved over onto the other end of the couch. Lifting my legs onto his lap, he took one of my feet and began kneading the muscles. His experienced fingers pushed and pulled one tender area then another. I knew he shared both my frustration and the helplessness to eliminate it.

"What would I do without you, Big D?" I sighed, allowing myself to relax contentedly for the moment.

Don shrugged. "I wish there was something more I could do."

"You know there's not." Since Lauren's birth, the month before, he had helped alleviate my burden by playing with Jane, washing dishes, folding laundry. He had eagerly participated in the formula feedings. But I had insisted on nursing during the middle of the night. Don had to get up and go to work early every morning.

"Do you think I'm becoming obsessed?" I pointed to the infant scales sitting on our country french buffet in the adjoining living room. "Every morning before I get her dressed, I bring her out to see if she's gained even a fraction of a pound. I'm beginning to dread our weekly appointments at the clinic. I'm sure they think I'm nuts — your typical overprotective mother."

"You're not nuts," Don exchanged one of my feet for the other. "You're a mom. And you love your little girl. You've spent every second of the day and night worrying about her since she was born."

"Not every second," I suddenly felt defensive, aware that my focus on Lauren had nearly excluded my attentiveness toward

Don and Jane.

"I understand, Terry. I'm not condemning you. You've had to be on an ongoing feeding frenzy. It's not supposed to be that way. And, don't forget, it's not like you're a complete novice. You've had one child already. No, you're not nuts and you're not over-protective."

I hoped he was right. It was true that I couldn't quit wondering what was preventing our baby from gaining weight. "It's the diarrhea I don't understand. Why is it that everything goes in one end and out the other so fast? With all she eats, she ought to weigh about two hundred pounds by now."

"At least."

"But why aren't the doctors more concerned?"

"Terry, don't forget, these doctors are pretty knowledgeable people, too."

"Maybe so. But they're not listening to me. Like you say, I've watched her every single day of her life. They only see her for a few minutes now and then. I can't seem to get through to them that I know something's wrong."

"Maybe you won't have to. Maybe she'll just suddenly start coming around like they say she will."

"How long are you going to buy that, Don?" I glared, again feeling isolated and defensive.

"Hey, I'm on your side." He looked hurt.

"I'm sorry. I'm just tired. I know it's not you. But some days it seems like I'm the only one who thinks she's got a problem. I wonder if I'm overreacting. Then I get an even stronger feeling that if I don't keep racking my brain to figure out what's wrong, she isn't going to make it. All I know is something's got to change."

Six weeks after Lauren's birth, nothing had changed. I decided to take things into my own hands. I scoured our shelves for reference books. I borrowed more from friends. In the afternoon, *while the baby napped and Jane played in her room, I collected the pile of books and began to search for answers that would explain our infant's condition. I skimmed tables of contents for terms that might seem to fit. It was in an old reference book for parents that I discovered the phrase, "failure to thrive." It was mentioned as one of the symptoms of cystic fibrosis, a disease of the respiratory and digestive systems. Disease. The word itself sent a shock wave rippling through my body, leaving me feeling weak, cold, vulnerable. I reached for the phone to call Don at the office.*

"Hi." I tried to sound calm when he answered.

"Hey babe. What's up?"

"I think I've found something. I couldn't wait till you got home. It's bad news."

"What are you talking about?"

"I looked it up in a book. The baby is failing to thrive, isn't she? Doesn't that sound like what she's doing?"

I could hear Don taking a deep breath through the phone, the nature of my call sinking in. "Failure to thrive," he repeated the words slowly. "Yeah, I guess it does. So what does that mean?"

"Failure to thrive is a symptom of an inherited disease called cystic fibrosis." I whispered the words softly, fearful that saying them out loud would confirm the diagnosis.

"Cystic fibrosis? I've never even heard of that."

"There's more," I frantically scanned the paragraph. "Chronic diarrhea and a constant, dry cough."

"She has that, too," came the discouraged reply.

"One more thing," I added, my voice heavy. "Babies with cystic fibrosis taste salty. You've said that yourself — that she tastes like a salt lick."

"It's summertime in Oklahoma. Everybody probably tastes salty."

"I'm going to ask them to test her at the clinic. She's got an appointment tomorrow."

"That sounds reasonable to me," Don said sadly. "Cystic fibrosis," he repeated. An ominous silence loomed as the deathly calm before a storm. It was as if he'd pronounced a verdict. It was also his recognition that our baby was really in trouble. "Terry, you know I'm behind you one hundred percent."

The next day, however, the pediatrician shook her head at my suggestion. "Cystic fibrosis is a very serious disease. I don't believe Lauren's symptoms warrant the test. I think you're putting yourself through too much stress over this."

I felt hot and defensive, awkward and foolish. I was clearly butting my head against a brick wall. Why couldn't I find the words to express how terrified I felt? How hearing her say that cystic fibrosis was serious made my heart stand still? Why couldn't they run the test just to appease me? I left angry, frustrated and confused. That afternoon, I ran errands with my mother and shared my concerns with her. "Everything in me says there's something horribly wrong with this child. Look at her. She looks like one of those malnourished babies on television advertisements."

"She is awfully thin," my mother admitted.

"Thin?" I groaned. "There's nothing to this baby. Every inch she grows makes her look skinnier and scrawnier. She's about to fall off the growth charts completely." I visualized the paragraphs in the book I had read, convinced that my daughter was suffering the same symptoms as those associated with the disease called cystic fibrosis. "I just know she's sick, Mom. But I can't get the doctors to acknowledge even the possibility. I don't know what else to do."

My mother listened carefully before offering her advice. "You know, Terry, sometimes mothers know things that doctors can't *see. That's why you can't give up. You've got to keep on looking for the answer until you're satisfied you've found it."*

A few days later, an idea sprang to mind. I called the geneticist with whom we'd worked prior to having Jane, because of another problem that had been identified and, thankfully, resolved. In the process, we'd tested negatively for genetic diseases and so had dismissed the worry that our children would have any kind of inherited disorder. The phone felt heavy in my hand. I dialed the number slowly, afraid of the questions I was about to ask, the answers I was afraid I would hear.

"Hello?" The familiar heavy Turkish accent sounded as warm as I'd remembered.

"Dr. Say, this is Terry Detrich."

"Mrs. Detrich, how are you?"

"Well, not so good, actually. In fact, that's why I'm calling." I struggled to prevent emotion from taking control of my words and my voice. "You see, we've had another baby recently."

"Well, then, congratulations. There's a problem with this child?"

"I think so. I am afraid my baby has cystic fibrosis."

The sympathetic concern was apparent in his tone. "This is a very serious disease, Mrs. Detrich. What would make you think your child is sick?"

I explained how the symptoms in the book mirrored those our baby had. I could no longer hold back the tears. "I don't know what to do," I sobbed.

"Can you get in your car and bring her to me right now?" the kind doctor suggested. "I'll be happy to take a look at her. Maybe I can relieve your fears."

"Thank you so much," I gratefully accepted his offer. "We'll be there as soon as we can."

After calling Don, I rushed the children into the car and sped

*off to the medical center where Dr. Say worked. The minute he
set eyes on Lauren, I knew my instincts had been right.*

*And so, here we were barely a week later, I mused despon-
dently. Yes, in fact our world had crumbled during those three
months prior to our baby's diagnosis. As we pulled in the driveway, I realized ages had passed since my friends and I had rid-
den bikes down the familiar streets of Tulsa. I knew that my own
child might never know the kind of security that had padded my
adolescent falls. In fact, the only thing I had now was uncertainty. With trembling hands, I opened the door to begin our new
lives.*

Chapter 3

GRIEF-STRICKEN

he consultation with Dr. Kramer had taken a toll. I needed some time to think. Back home in our bedroom, I rummaged through drawers for a pair of shorts and socks. I laced up my running shoes and considered the likelihood of getting lucky enough to run myself into the ground.

I could hear Terry talking to Jane as she changed the baby in the next room. "See you girls later," I waved on my way to the door.

"Bye, Daddy," Jane ran over to hug my leg.

Terry blew a kiss, sensing the necessity of my mission. "Take your time."

I headed down the driveway to the street that ran in front of our house. I could feel the warmth of the midday sun on my back. The blue sky provided a brilliant backdrop for the festival of autumn color. On another day, I might have appreciated the beauty more fully. Miserable as I was from the morning's events, I barely took notice.

Having set a steady pace, I reviewed again the fact that life as I had known it was history. I didn't consider myself to be an exceptionally goal-driven person, but I did recall sometime before starting law school establishing a general idea of the direction I thought my life would take. I'd hoped to start my own firm, get married, have a couple of kids. I saw myself coaching ball games, playing catch in the yard and taking family vacations. I figured I'd marry a woman for life. My parents had been great role models in that regard.

Up until this morning, I reflected, I'd pretty well been on track with my plan. I'd started a law firm with a friend from school and business was growing as fast as we let it. I had married a beautiful woman and our relationship was stronger than ever. We'd had two little girls and I'd already bought Jane a leather baseball mitt.

The realization that the baby had an incurable disease rendered every expectation and achievement I'd had meaningless. Regardless of my own efforts to be a stellar husband and father, or a successful businessman, I knew I could do absolutely nothing to protect my child from the illness that had already almost taken her from us. I felt utterly hopeless. I ran harder.

For three months, Terry had been so certain there was something wrong, nursing Lauren around the clock, enduring the pediatricians' criticism at the weekly clinic visits. I recalled how she had first identified cystic fibrosis, yet been rebuffed by doctors who turned a deaf ear. It had taken too long for me to become convinced as well. I vowed to listen more carefully to my wife in the future.

The sweat poured down my body as my feet pounded the pavement. But no matter how hard I ran, I couldn't outpace the weight that had settled on my shoulders in the doctor's office. I wasn't a quitter anyway. I was the husband, the father — and my family needed me. I couldn't let them down. As Dr. Kramer had said, being a caregiver would be time-consuming. Expenses would be high.

There would be other challenges, too. Sharing the task of caring for a child with a life-threatening disease was undoubtedly going to affect my marriage. There would be constant worry, strain. Would we be able to handle it? I was thankful that I loved my wife. And what about Jane? Her life would be forever changed, too. Would she become another victim of the statistics Dr. Kramer had rattled off?

Too many questions. Too many unknowns. Finally, exhaustion began to replace nervous energy. I had come up with no answers but it was time to go home.

Having fed the baby and put her down for a nap, I began the next task, automatically spreading peanut butter, banana and honey on a piece of wheatberry bread. I cut it in quarters and placed it on a plate with a few red grapes. I stuck a straw in a box of juice, grabbed a napkin — black and orange jack-o-lanterns with bright yellow teeth. It was almost Halloween. "Janie, lunch is ready, honey." I wondered — whose tired, sad voice is that, anyway?

Sturdy little legs tucked into tennis shoes with socks trimmed in purple came trudging in the kitchen. I brushed little wisps of blonde hair away from her face. The purple sateen ribbon I'd so carefully tied this morning had long ago slipped down the silky strands of ponytail. I picked up my tow-headed cherub, whose toddler-sized roundness evinced vitality and health. I felt the need to hold her and to tell her how happy I was that she was okay. That she was healthy. That I could count on her to do all the things that little girls should do. Like grow up.

"I love you, mommy," she chirped, delighting in my atten-tion. I realized how distracted I had been since Lauren's birth. It was hard enough for the older child to adjust to a new sibling, but for months Jane's momma had been preoccupied with the sur-vival of a human being. I hugged her tighter.

"I love you, too."

"Anybody home?" The front door opened. My mother walked in, carrying a bag of groceries she'd picked up for us at the store. Setting them on the counter, she glanced at me momentarily, silently, sadly, acknowledging the burden that Don and I now car-ried.

"Amma! Can we go feed the swans?" Jane squealed happily.

"Sshh! Jane, the baby is asleep," I pleaded. Lauren had slept all morning, awakening only long enough to eat. Still, I craved the time to sort through what I had heard, what our predicament was.

"There's nothing I'd rather do in the whole wide world!" My mom had long ago mastered the art of grand-parenting. She set the bag down and turned to me. "I am so very sorry, honey," she offered, eyes glistening.

"Me, too." I put my arms around her and wished that I were once again Jane's age and that my mother could make everything all better.

Slurping up the last of her juice, Jane climbed down. "I'm done. Let's go Amma! Bye Momma."

"Hang on, there, little lady." I wet a warm washcloth and tenderly painted back the fresh-faced roses where peanut butter had been smeared. "Have fun, sweetie." I waved, swallowing back tears for the millionth time.

Alone once more, I brushed the crumbs off the kitchen table. It felt so strange to admit that our child, who had yet to roll over, take a step, or say "Momma," was fighting for her life. It was overwhelming to think that Don and I would be such a huge part of her support system. How does one deal with a situation like this? It's not like there are a lot of precedents out there that you see every day. No convenient reference books describe how parents should watch as their child slowly deteriorates and dies.

Plus, I thought, I was used to going to doctors who could make me well. You get sick. They give you a pill. You get better. The next time you get sick, you call them, confident that they can do the same thing. But Dr. Kramer couldn't make our baby well. There was no pill to make cystic fibrosis go away.

The impact of those words crushed my spirit. I desperately needed something to hope for. I reflected on an incident that had happened several nights before. Lauren and I had gone to a local take-out restaurant to pick up some dinner. While I was waiting for the order, I sat looking at my child, grief-stricken.

What had I done to cause my baby to be wasting away? Was I being punished for something I had done in my past? Something so despicable that the misery of an infant would be considered just? How could such an innocent child be made to suffer through life? I felt inadequate to care for a critically ill baby. How could I take care of her special needs? How long would I have her? There was not a satisfactory answer for any of my questions. I was working myself into a frenzy.

Then something extraordinary happened. I looked down at my tiny little daughter. Since her birth, there had been something exquisite about her sea-blue eyes. They had an almost ethereal quality. Lately, she had withdrawn; I was sure in order to concentrate on sheer survival. But now, as I looked again into her beautiful eyes, I didn't see any suffering, no vacant gaze of a starving infant. In fact, I felt a calm sense of peacefulness. At that moment a seed of hope seemed to plant itself within me. It was as if God was comforting me, saying, "This little girl is mine. I will take care of her forever."

As I finished rinsing the lunch dishes, I realized the incredible nature of this experience. Did I really, honestly believe that God would send me a personal message? Or were my mind, my heart and my soul creating a dream out of my desperation? It didn't really matter. It was the single thread of hope I had. I wasn't about to let go.

Chapter 4

ADJUSTMENTS

"That'll be six hundred dollars, Mr. Detrich," the pharmacist at the drug store announced, somewhat apologetically. I'd delivered the prescriptions and told her about our morning's news.

"You've got to be kidding!" I was stunned. "For a few bottles of pills and some baby formula?" I picked up one of the containers of formula and pointed to the label. "It says it's pre-digested right here on the can. Doesn't that entitle us to get some sort of a discount?"

She smiled, then shrugged. "I'm afraid that's something you're going to have to get used to with CF." Handing her my credit card, I wondered what our limit was, thinking we'd have to see about raising it soon. I grabbed the bag and headed home.

Terry was in the kitchen holding Lauren, setting out a jar of baby fruit and an empty bottle. "She's hungry." As soon as Terry started mixing the formula with the water, we all groaned.

"Doesn't smell quite as bad as the regular brand," I said. "It smells twice as bad." I searched the bags for one of the little bottles of capsules. "Let's see if these million dollar enzymes help fill her up." Terry put some baby fruit on a spoon. I fumbled around trying to twist off the gelatin covering. Then I carefully sprinkled the inside of half a capsule onto the fruit.

"Yuck!" Jane said looking at the odd spheres. "What's that stuff?"

"We hope this medicine will help your little sister grow," Terry explained. "She is very, very hungry. This will be the first time she's had anything other than milk."

"I'm hungry, too, Mommy." Jane said.

"Not now, Jane. It's the baby's turn."

"Down the hatch!" I tried to sound encouraging as Terry lifted the spoon to Lauren's mouth. Incredibly, she welcomed the contents, medicine and all.

"She likes it," Jane said wonderingly. "Give her some more."

"Let's try this milk first," Terry suggested, cradling the baby in one arm and the bottle in the other. Lauren needed no urging. Immediately, she began to drink. Within minutes, she had guzzled the entire bottle.

"Don, did you notice?" Terry asked me, smiling for the first time in days.

"What?"

"I didn't have to change her diaper in the middle of the bottle."

"Hey," I smiled back. "You're right. At least it hasn't gone in one end and immediately out the other." Nearly three days passed before she had another bowel movement.

Dr. Kramer had been right — he had certainly given us enough to do. The formula prescribed adhered to the bottom of bottles like cement. It took forever to dislodge the residue and get them as clean as we thought they should be to prevent bacteria from growing. I tried to help Terry when I could, cleaning or mixing formula or feeding the baby. Of course, that wasn't the extent of it. We had to get used to the idea of giving her the enzymes every single time she ate or drank. More than once we found ourselves rushing home from a restaurant to grab the enzymes we'd left behind. We'd had three months to witness what happened when she didn't take them.

It wasn't long before the enzymes, vitamins and minerals began to work their magic on our little girl. Within six weeks of her diagnosis, she had filled up and out. She began to take in everything that was happening around her and to develop in a normal pattern, reaching out, rolling over, pulling up.

Jane was as thrilled as we were at the evidence her baby sister was becoming more responsive. With Lauren in her infant seat, Jane had a captive, but appreciative audience to entertain. "Look, Daddy, she's laughing at me. I can make her laugh!"

"Yeah. How about that?"

"Pat-a-cake, pat-a-cake, baker's man," Jane would sing and play the baby's little hands as if Lauren was an obedient marionette. Lauren's laugh was contagious from the start, low and husky and full. Jane's attentions would prompt both girls into giggles that were a welcome interruption from the strange, sad world to which we were adjusting.

I found myself torn more than ever between the two realms in which I lived. I was honing my skills as a real estate attorney, enjoying the thrill of putting together complicated, million-dollar acquisitions. At the same time, I was drawn toward this little family of mine in a way that I had never been. I felt guilty that I could escape to the office, leaving Terry at home with all the new responsibilities of caring for a baby with special needs. I didn't know how long we would have Lauren, how long we would get to be a family. As her health appeared to improve, I wondered how long it would be before it once again deteriorated as the disease found another avenue to parade through her body. I didn't want to miss the fleeting good times.

Before Lauren, I did all the things I'd looked forward to when I decided to become a stay-at-home mom. I hoped that the time I was able to spend with our children would enable me to be more than just a housekeeper or chauffeur. I wanted to be there for them when they needed a listening ear, or a word of advice, or just a hug. I wanted to be there for the good days and the bad, to pass along our ideas of right and wrong, values we thought were critical. We hoped that our home would be the kind of place that any member of our family would want to be. Unfortunately, with the advent of cystic fibrosis, there were many times it was a place I didn't want to be.

Instead of being enthralled by the achievements of my little girls, I was engrossed in learning how to administer medications, manage a limited insurance policy, and diligently watch my baby for signs of illness. I had to become a vigilante, afraid of missing a single pill or dose of medication, afraid of missing a clue that cystic fibrosis might leave. I knew that the insurance money was like cash to us, with a million dollar lifetime cap for each person, and I felt compelled to keep track of every dollar claimed. There were many days when, overwhelmed by the responsibility, I felt the urge to escape.

"Mom, do you think you could have a little company this afternoon?" I asked my mother frequently. "I'd just like to run a few errands — by myself."

I longed for peace and quiet. I never had the satisfaction that I was even a step ahead. I thought if I could just get in my car — alone — or run to the store — alone — maybe then I could make sense of whether or not I was accomplishing anything. I didn't want to leave at night, though I'm sure Don would have been more than willing. By then I was too tired. I was always tired, but rarely sleepy. And so, I'd leave the girls in the middle of the day with my mother, Lauren with her enzymes, and Jane with her boundless energy.

I knew most mothers needed a break. But I sensed it was not as much a break from my kids I sought as it was a separation from the constant reminder of cystic fibrosis. In addition to the time it took was the knowledge that no matter how diligent I was, I couldn't protect my child from the disease. I grieved that Lauren, herself, could never get away. The burden was part of her. Inside, it was disease, and outside it took the form of a constant medical regimen. Still, there were many days when I left in order to temporarily escape — catching my breath before I took the burden back on again.

I made believe there were valid purposes to my outings. Things that needed to be done. Errands that had to be accomplished. Sadly, for Don, most of these errands were costly. Most of the time I returned home, having to again take on the burden of CF, with the added burden of guilt for having spent money that didn't need to be spent.

In the midst of our efforts to make sense of our child's illness as well as the impact it was having on our lives, we discovered the resourcefulness and sensitivity of our extended family and friends. Cards and letters, phone calls and visits were a constant source of encouragement to us. "Hey guys. We're thinking about you. If there's anything we can do, let us know," was a consistent refrain. We were on prayer lists all over the country.

"My mother-in-law who lives in Phoenix has asked her Sunday School class to include Lauren in their intentions," was another typical message.

One of the letters we received made a permanent impression. We had chosen the name Lauren Chevalier Detrich. It was a family name and we liked its long and flowing beauty, but somehow it didn't end up fitting our miniature little girl. Don has a penchant for giving people nicknames. He hadn't been able to think of one that seemed just right for our baby. Then my sister sent us a letter. She mentioned that in the last chapter of the Book of Matthew, there is a verse that says, "And lo, I will be with you always . . ." The comfort of that phrase struck a responsive chord. Lauren became "Lo" as a hopeful reminder that she was not alone in her struggle.

We shared this story with Lo when she was very young. Somehow, when she heard it, she assumed there was an additional twist to the message. For many years, she thought that the bible verse had been addressed specifically to her.

Chapter 5

FIRST
INFECTION

The inevitable first respiratory infection hit just before New Year's when Lo was six months old. The runny nose and dry hacking cough that all little kids have from time to time evolved into fits of retching, with only seconds in between sieges. Plans to celebrate with friends were cancelled as we decided to stay at home and monitor Lo's condition. It could have been a fair warning of the demise of our social lives for the next decade and a half.

"Time for bed, Jane," Terry announced, picking up the fading blanket that accompanied Jane everywhere. "Let's go."

Jane slowly pushed herself up, eyeing her little sister, sitting on my lap. "Why isn't Lo going to go, too?"

"She's kind of sick tonight," I tried to explain. "Mom and I are going to watch her for a while."

"Hmmm," Jane answered, obviously unconvinced. Putting

her hands on her hips, she tilted her head and grinned hopefully. "I could stay up and watch her with you."

Immediately, Lo began to cough again, as she worked unsuccessfully to rid herself of the congestion in her lungs. The distressing sound heightened the tension I felt. Out of the corner of my eye, I caught Terry cringing. I shook my head at Jane. The last thing I needed was an argument from a three-year-old. "No, that's okay, Jane. I think we can make it." Knowing her single-minded desire was to join Lo on my lap, I offered, "C'mon, Lo, let's all go say good night to your big sister."

We followed Jane back to her room and sat on her bed while she climbed under her covers and arranged a stack of picture books by her side. After going through the ritual of our nightly prayers, which were sandwiched in between Lo's coughing spells, Jane made a last request. "Family hug, Daddy?"

"You betcha, Jazz-o," I agreed. I pulled her into a sitting position. Terry wrapped one arm around Jane and the other around me and Lo. "One-two-three!" we shouted in unison.

"Happy New Year, sweetie," Terry kissed Jane and straightened her covers once more. Again, Lo started coughing. "I'll take her now," Terry offered, lifting Lo out of my arms. "We're going to go get a little more cough medicine."

"Good night, Janie," I squeezed the little hand reaching up for mine. "We'll see you tomorrow."

"If I get scared can I come out with you and Mommy?" Jane asked.

"We'll be right here if you need us, Jane. But there's no reason for you to come out. Mom and I need a while to talk by ourselves."

"But Lo is going to be with you, Daddy," Jane insisted.

Why is it that little kids have to have an answer for everything, I wondered. I was tired, I wanted a few minutes to at least talk to my wife, I was worried about the cough that I already heard again coming from the den and I wondered if Lo was ever going to get to sleep. This was not the way I'd intended to usher in the New Year. Not even close.

"Jane, I said good night. And I meant it." The tone in my voice was becoming far less conciliatory than it had been. "Can't you hear Lo coughing? Don't you realize that if we could put her to sleep right now we would? This whole deal is tough on all of us. You're just going to have to trust us when things don't seem fair."

I decided my explanations weren't going to get any further with Jane than they already had. She was only three years old. We couldn't expect her to realize that now we had a critical illness in the family, her efforts to manipulate us would have to stop. We couldn't expect her to adjust her own fears and needs according to the situation. But, we also couldn't accommodate them as we might have if Lo had been healthy. It was time to leave. I found Terry pacing the floor with Lo who was heaving violently from head to toe. "Whenever I hear that cough, it rips my guts out," I said miserably.

"Me too, Big D. It's hard to believe a little baby can make these awful sounds. I don't know what else to do. I've taken her to Dr. Kramer twice already. She's on antibiotics, Prednisone, and cough medicine. Surely it's going to take effect eventually. He said we have to be careful about giving her Prednisone, by the way. It's got some dangerous side effects."

"Like what?"

She waited till the next round of coughing subsided. "Like bone pain, vision problems, or arthritis."

"Great. That's just great, isn't it? You give her one thing to help her and cause her more problems for later on."

"What choice do we have, Don? He also said that if she coughs too long and too hard, she runs the risk of having a lung collapse."

"Poor little kid," I looked at Lo, coughing away, oblivious to the implications of her prognosis. She caught me looking at her and smiled. It broke my heart — again. "It's just not fair," I said, closing my eyes.

Terry and I took turns holding Lo for the next hour. We could have put her in her crib but we didn't want her to feel she had to endure the coughing alone. Finally, the arsenal of medications began to take affect. Her eyes grew heavy and the coughing less harsh. Just before midnight, we carried her in to her bedroom and laid her down, hoping that at least for a few hours, she would be able to stay asleep.

"Happy New Year, Terry," I said as we fell into our own bed.

"Sure," she replied through a yawn.

I turned the lights out, wondering if there was even the slightest possibility that the coming weeks could hold the promise of happier times.

Chapter 6

FIRST
HOSPITAL STAY

*O*n top of the respiratory infection, Lo
contracted an intestinal virus a week
later. "It seems like we're in a vicious
cycle," I explained to Dr. Kramer wearily. "We can't even get
rid of one infection before another jumps in. What's our next
step?"

"We can put her in the hospital," he answered pragmati-
cally. "We don't want her to get dehydrated from the diarrhea.
This particular virus has been virulent this year. We're having
quite a problem with it. It's the kind of rotavirus that runs ram-
pant through third world countries. Because it's highly contagious, I would put her in isolation at the hospital. At the same
time, we can give her IV's for her bronchial infection."

We had spent the past several months celebrating Lo's weight
gains. The last thing we needed was for her to lose the precious
pounds we had worked so hard to put on. "How long will she

have to be in the hospital?" I asked.

"I can't tell you," Dr. Kramer said. "It's a case-by-case situation. The average stay is three weeks."

Three weeks sounded like an eternity. Jane's fourth birthday was three weeks away. I wondered if we'd be out by then. But I also knew I could do no more at home. My patience and energy had hit a new low. "Okay, let's do it," I said. "Just tell us where and when to check in."

After the arrangements were made, I called Don and told him the news. "I'll meet you at home in an hour," he said. "We'll all go together."

I gathered up toys and books to occupy the girls. I really had no idea what we'd need in a hospital for an extended period. I'd never been in this situation. The empty feeling that I'd experienced so intensely the day Dr. Kramer told us about Lo's prognosis had come back with a vengeance. So this was how it was going to be, I thought. In and out of the hospital for weeks at a time. I was relieved to hear Don's car pull into the garage.

He walked in and kissed Jane and me and then picked Lo up and hugged her tightly. "My sweet little woman," was all he said. That's what he called her when his heart was too full to say anything else. We picked up the bags and loaded the back of the station wagon.

"Why don't you spend the night at the hospital tonight, babe?" Don suggested. "I'll stay at home with Jane. Tomorrow we can switch. That way, we'll each get a decent sleep every other night."

"And we'll get to spend some time alone with Jane," I added. "This is going to be hard on her. She could be bored to death at the hospital." I pulled out a couple of toiletries, nightgown and change of clothes. Suddenly, I just wanted to get there. The sooner we started this process, I figured, the sooner we'd be back home again.

After checking in and enduring the insertion of an IV catheter into Lo's wrist, Don and Jane left for the night. I tried to organize the room in as friendly a manner as I could, sticking stuffed animals in crib corners and leaning books against windowsills. This was a rather difficult task as I surveyed the stainless steel crib bars, the intravenous apparatus pumping medicines and liquid through feet upon feet of tubing and into Lo, and the typically sterile décor of a hospital room.

Finally, I could think of nothing that had been left undone. Lo had eaten and been changed. She'd had all of her evening oral medications. The IV was infusing. It was strange to think that even if the alarm went off, it wouldn't be my job to take care of Lo. A nurse would come in to attend to the problem. I had grown used to hovering over this baby, feeling responsible for each and every detail regarding her medical needs.

She was lying comfortably in her infant seat. I had made up the cot that was to be my bed for the night. I realized that since her birth, I had been consumed by my efforts to help her gain weight, to watch for signs of infections, to follow each and every instruction that Dr. Kramer had prescribed. I had been taking as good care of her as I thought possible. But once again, I looked into those blue, oh-so-blue eyes. It occurred to me that somewhere during the course of these last six months, this little baby had learned to smile. She was smiling at me now. In fact, I realized that she'd been smiling at me for months — innocently, lovingly. I had been so preoccupied with making sure she survived and so fearful I might lose her that I had somehow remained a little distant. She had not.

In the midst of all the turmoil, she had patiently waited for me. And now, as her tiny hands reached out to be held, I was ready. I picked my baby up and held her, as if for the very first time. We spent the next few hours getting to know each other. Not as patient and caregiver, but as mother and child. We laughed and played as mothers and their babies are meant to do. And I knew that whatever the cost, this little girl had captured my heart forever.

In between intravenous infusions, the rest of the hospital stay was filled with technicians running a variety of tests on Lo. Each time they came to get her they brought along a huge gurney. It reminded me of my own terror of having my tonsils out when I was three years old.

Hospital regulations of the 1950's prevented my mother from being able to accompany me to the surgery room. I had vivid recollections of the nurse in her starched white uniform and hat leading the way down the endless corridors, as a dark-headed, burly technician wheeled the stretcher. I knew I was headed for surgery but I wasn't quite sure what that meant. So far, it had involved my being plucked away from my mother's comforting and protective eye. At one point, they stopped to talk to someone. I decided this was my chance. I slipped off the side of the stretcher and raced down the hall to try and find my mom, only to be recaptured by the nurse who severely reprimanded me. Moments later, I was laid down on an operating table screaming. A mask was placed over my mouth and nose. This memory had left me with a lasting aversion to hospitals and the people who ran them.

Knowing that Lo was going to have to undergo innumerable medical procedures, I decided I would have to lay aside my own fears and memories after nearly thirty years. At the same time, I was determined to do everything I could to prevent her from being as terrified as I had been. Whenever they came to get her, I asked if I could come along. Thankfully, they always obliged. Thankfully, too, my baby was trusting, even at six months. Her ready smile captivated the nurses and aides, x-ray specialists and therapists. I couldn't help but think their gentle handling of my baby and thoughtful explanations to me were God's way of reminding me that he was indeed keeping the promise he had made to me that night at the drive-in restaurant before Lo's diagnosis.

"Dr. Kramer, how bad a case of CF does she have?" I asked him after the results were compiled.

"I'm sorry, I really can't answer that question."

"But do the x-rays indicate her lungs are already damaged?" I had no doubt established myself as a pest, but I was hoping he'd be able to say something that would assuage my fears.

"The tests we've been running will establish a base for the future," he explained. "We'll know more when we have comparisons to make than we do now."

I couldn't tell whether he was trying to avoid my question or if he was just trying to be objective. I had discovered that Dr. Kramer was not one to speculate. He based his decisions on statistics and facts rather than on subjective opinions just to sweeten the story. It was something else to which Don and I simply had to adjust.

Chapter 7

DÉJÀ VU

"**M**y dear Lo-Lo. Please know you will always be my sweet little woman. I've been where you are. There were no guarantees I was going to make it either. But no matter what happens, you can be sure your mother and I will do whatever we can for you. I promise you that."

I whispered in a voice so soft I could barely hear it. Slipping my hand through the bars on the crib, I gently squeezed my sleeping baby's tiny fist. Tears welled in my eyes as if the sadness which shrouded me could no longer contain them. I realized the helplessness I felt was surely akin to what my parents had experienced. How long ago had it been? I was only eight years old when it all started. I closed my eyes and reached for the memories — deeper and further than usual. Over and over my mother and father had told me the story. I had heard through the ears of a child. Now, as I contemplated the events that had transpired so long ago, I began for the first time, to understand what it was I had faced, and what it was that my family had endured.

◌ ◌ ◌

Winter had blanketed Chicago's suburbs in white that February in 1960. After-school snowball fights determined rank in the neighborhood. Merciless icy missiles met their fur-trimmed targets, triggering secondary hoots of laughter from behind hedges of evergreen.

"OK, boys. That's it." This command from headquarters — my mother's voice — was the only authoritative edict that could stop our battle. It signaled dinnertime. Fifteen minutes later, my dad, George Detrich, trudged up the driveway, having walked the usual route home from the train station. Already sitting in the kitchen, watching our mother put food on the table in front of us, my two brothers and I waited impatiently.

As soon as we could see him through the kitchen window, we shouted, "Hey, Dad! We're starving!"

"Boys, give your father a minute to get in the door," Mom laughed. It was a nightly ritual, full of the kind of routine that builds a sense of familiarity and secure expectation. Five minutes later, Dad's boots were drying next to ours in the tiny utility room next to the kitchen. My father had settled himself comfortably at the head of the table.

Dinnertime was always an enjoyable event in those days. Amidst the clatter of forks on china, my older brother, Jeff, grinned and looked at me. Holding up his index finger, he teased, "How many fingers do you see?"

My little brother, Bobby, and I both covered one of our eyes. Bobby mischievously studied Jeff's outstretched finger, then dramatically announced, "I see two fingers!" Everybody laughed except me.

Dad noticed my puzzled expression first. "What's the

matter, Donny?"

I rubbed my eyes, and blinked. "I couldn't tell how many fingers Jeff was holding up. I can't see anything out of that eye."

"What!" Startled, Mom and Dad looked at me.

Mom leaned over to peer closely at the eye. "Maybe you've gotten something in it." Taking my face in her hands she inspected one eye and then the other.

"I don't think so."

"Here, son. Let's cover your eye again," Dad insisted. He held his hand over my right eye. My world became dark. "Now what do you see?"

"Nothing. I told you, I can't see a thing."

"I'll call Dr. Scott this very minute," Mom twisted around quickly and reached for the phone book in the drawer behind her. I know she was trying to sound calm but I could see her finger shaking as she scanned down the pages looking for our family doctor's number. He agreed to see me early the next morning.

My dad had a habit of having one or two cigarettes at the kitchen table after dinner every night. He didn't consider himself a smoker. He'd merely enjoyed the ritual for years. The evening we discovered my blindness, he stayed at the table longer than usual, tapping the ashes emphatically on the elephant ashtray, the only one my mother allowed in the house. While he smoked, my mother washed the dishes. I sat at the table and watched them both. "Have you ever noticed this before, Don?" He asked as he watched the thin line of smoke lazily make its way upward.

I tried to recall the past few days and weeks. "No, not till tonight." I shook my head.

"Are you sure you didn't get hit by a snowball today?"

"I'm sure. I'd remember that, Dad. Pretty weird, huh?" My

mother dried her hands with a dishtowel as she looked out the window. It was long after the sun had gone down. There was nothing to see.

"Yes, it is very strange," my dad said. "But I'm sure we'll get it figured out, Donny. There's probably a simple explanation." With those words of assurance, I pushed back my chair and left the room. But I still remember my parents' talking quietly at the table long after I'd left.

The next morning Dr. Scott examined my eye carefully. "You need to take Don to an ophthalmologist right away. I don't know what has caused this sudden blindness but it needs to be diagnosed immediately."

The ophthalmologist he sent us to had no answer either. "There's no obvious reason why Don would lose the vision out of his left eye. I'm afraid what we're dealing with is beyond my expertise. Fortunately, we do have one of the world's renowned eye clinics right here in Chicago. There are other places you could go, but I'd recommend Dr. Frank Newell over anyone in the United States. If you'd like, I'll call and arrange an appointment for you myself. I'll tell him you need to be seen as soon as possible."

The next morning we headed downtown on the Illinois Central. I loved getting to ride the train that my dad took to work every day. Dr. Newell's office was at the Bobs Roberts Hospital associated with the University of Chicago. After examining my eye, his concerns mirrored those of the other doctors we'd seen. Suddenly, I found myself on display — looking up, looking down, looking right and looking left for a myriad of medical students under the doctor's tutelage. Each shone a flashlight into the eye, peering for some sign that would explain my blindness.

It took several appointments, as well as an assortment of

lab work before the medical team could reach even a preliminary diagnosis. Finally, Dr. Newell suggested a more invasive procedure in which some fluid would be drawn from the eye. It would require me to stay in the hospital for a couple of days, but he thought it might provide more conclusive evidence.

The days turned into weeks. Mom and Dad tried to guard their feelings around us boys, but I noticed they spent a lot more time talking alone than usual. I could tell my mother looked tired and my dad often seemed preoccupied. Ignorance and fear must have been threatening foes, particularly since the cause and consequence of my blindness had not been determined. "We'll just have to wait and see a little longer," they'd say, as much to convince themselves as me.

Aside from the ever-increasing sense of frustration and anxiety, I now know there were financial concerns. Dad's job as an accountant for Commonwealth Edison provided a modest income. However, he and Mom both knew that a catastrophic illness could wipe them out, even with the utility company's insurance benefits.

In spite of my parents' worries, I wasn't particularly upset about my situation. I hadn't been in pain. I hadn't even felt sick. Absences from school in the past had only been allowed for fever or nausea. I'd gotten to miss school and take the train to the city. On days when Mom drove me in our car, we'd stop for my favorite treat — a chocolate milkshake with an extra scoop of vanilla ice cream. As far as I was concerned, as long as I could see out of one eye — what difference did the blindness make?

"Don has a rare form of cancer called retinal blastoma," was Dr. Newell's disheartening answer following the procedure to withdraw fluid from my eye. "The cancer can affect one eye — or even both of them. So far, Don has only lost sight in his left eye. We'll have to remove it immediately." He allowed this news to sink in for a minute before going on. "We may have to remove both of them if we find the cancer has spread. And if it has reached the optic nerve," he spoke very slowly and quietly, "there will be nothing left for us to do." He looked at all of us sympathetically. "I'm so sorry."

I listened carefully to every word he said. Then, I looked over at my mom and saw the tears streaming down her face. Somehow, I still knew I'd be all right, that my job now was to comfort my mother. I walked over to her and put my arm around her. "It's okay, Mom. I don't need that old eye, anyway. I can see out of the other one just fine."

My surgery was scheduled for two days later. Mom and Dad no doubt dreaded what lay ahead for me. At the least, I would have to spend the rest of my life with only one eye. Or, I could lose both and be blind. They weren't prepared to consider the worst scenario, or at least they never mentioned it.

Coping with tragedy was familiar to Dad. When he was eight, he had lost his mother and a younger sibling during childbirth. His father had died of pneumonia just a few years later. By the time he was seventeen, in the midst of The Great Depression, Dad had moved into a Chicago YMCA, working to support himself and his little brother. Eventually, an aunt took in his little brother and Dad was left to fend for himself. Consequently, my mother and we boys were his only real family. The comfort and security of his wife and children had filled the void left by his childhood.

Now, a new tragedy loomed. I was too young to fully appreciate what was happening to me, but, for some reason, I continued to feel a calm acceptance. Dad did all he could to encourage me. I still remember his words. "You'll get through this surgery just fine, Donny. You know the saying we live by:

My name is Detrich. Give me the toughest job you've got."

Though she didn't show it, Mom, no doubt, was devastated by my prognosis. Her mother had died of cancer when she was growing up. She used to talk about how sad it was that her mother had died so young. The knowledge that I now faced the same dreaded disease must have terrified her. But she kept a cheerful smile on her face and acted as if everything was still pretty normal around our house.

My older brother, Jeff, took the news of my impending surgery harder than anybody — at least on the outside. He was eleven at the time and had always been interested in reading and learning. After my diagnosis, he became quieter than usual. He read everything he could get his hands on about cancer. Fortunately for everybody, Bobby was too young to have any idea about what was going on. His happy-go-lucky demeanor provided us all with at least a little comic relief.

I remember being anxious to get the surgery over with so I could start playing ball again. Still, I wasn't quite prepared for the team of nurses that marched into my hospital room early that April morning in 1960. One carried a hypodermic needle that looked big enough to launch a spaceship into orbit.

Mom and Dad went down to the pre-surgery area with me, no doubt wondering if they'd ever see me alive again or if I'd ever be able to see them. During the many waiting periods we'd been through, we had developed a signal. Three little squeezes of the hand meant, "I love you." Already partially under from the sedative I'd been given, I sent each of my parents the familiar silent message as the orderly came to wheel me away.

Nine long hours must have been excruciating for my parents as they sat in the waiting room to hear my fate. My mother, a devout Roman Catholic, had been praying unceasingly since we'd discovered my problem. Now, she had nothing but faith to cling to for solace. Dad told me later he had wondered if it would be better for me to die than to live my life in total darkness. I was an athletic little kid. He was afraid I would be devastated not to be able to develop my potential.

After what had seemed like an eternity, Dr. Newell appeared with news that was as good as could be expected. "He came through the operation well," he said with a tired but encouraging smile. "We had to remove the left eye but the cancer doesn't appear to have spread. We'll continue to watch it closely, to make sure nothing shows up in the right eye or elsewhere. But for the time being, I'd say you have a lot to be happy about." Exhausted, elated and relieved, Mom and Dad said they shook the doctor's hand and then hugged one another as the silent tears of thankfulness fell.

Hours later, in the pediatric ward, I woke up. I had never been hungrier in my life. "I'll eat anything!" I promised. As soon as my dinner tray was placed in front of me, I attacked it. It didn't matter that I had just survived a nine-hour operation during which my life was in jeopardy. It didn't matter that my entire head was wrapped in bandages to cover the socket where my left eye had once been. All I cared about was eating. Even my least favorite green peas tasted wonderful.

I had to spend the next several days recuperating in the hospital. Most of the time, I was without my parents. The hospital was more than an hour away from our suburban home and my brothers were under visiting age. When Mom and Dad came to see me, they had to find a sitter for Jeff and Bobby or leave them with my aunt who lived in another suburb.

It was the first time in my life I had been away from home. As the days wore on, I became homesick and lonely for my family. The nights were even harder, especially when a spring storm set off clashes of thunder. Usually, I occupied myself by playing with the other boys in the ward.

Sometimes, we would open our window and yell at the passersby on the street below. We occupied ourselves playing cards for hours. I became an expert at shuffling and making a "bridge" with the deck. But the highlight of my hospital stay was riding around in a wheelchair. Being the sports-minded type, I organized races down the corridors. Careening down the hallways was exciting, even though it left a few permanent indentations in the walls and doors. It was only when I mastered the art of "wheelies" that the nurses banned me from further wheelchair exhibitions.

Finally, Dr. Newell was ready to discharge me. "We'll have to track Don's progress for the next ten years," he counseled us as he sat at the end of my hospital bed. "Because of the rarity of his case, what with it showing up so late in childhood, we won't be confident that we're out of the woods till then. We feel certain that we got all the cancer but there's still a high risk it will show up in the other eye." Looking at me, he said, "The first six months will be the most critical, son, so we'll be seeing you often. But then the visits will taper off."

He went on to outline other ramifications of my surgery. I would have no depth perception. Many of the things I had done before might be extremely frustrating and difficult. He suggested I might be self-conscious about having only one eye, that I might not want to go back to school until the next year, which would be perfectly normal.

"Just be patient with him," Dr. Newell told my parents. "Don't push him. And try not to let him play too hard for a while. That could cause additional bleeding. Once the tissue heals, he can be fitted with a prosthesis."

Dr. Newell smiled at me as he rose to leave. "Don, you've

been a terrific patient. You're a real fighter." He shook my hand, and then turned to my parents. "My congratulations to you both. I know this ordeal has been stressful but your support of your son is obvious. He is fortunate to be a part of such a loving family. That can make all the difference." He extended his hand to my dad and then took my mom's hand in both of his. "Marie, I'll look forward to watching your son grow up."

Once again I noticed the tears streaming down my mother's face but this time I knew they were tears of happiness. Now, the time had come for me to figure out how to cope with my new challenge. My parents were no doubt eager to regain some sense of normalcy. Meanwhile, we would continue to wait and see if the cancer would rear its ugly head again.

Years later my mother told me the dilemma she and dad continued to face. "I'll quit my job," dad offered. "Don needs to have the opportunity to see the world. What if he ends up losing his other eye? This may be his only chance."

My mom was adamant in her own stance. "Donny doesn't care about traveling, honey," she stood firm. "He just wants to do the things other little boys do. We have to think about what is best for our family. If you quit your job, what would we live on? We have to eat, George. And we have Bobby and Jeff to think about as well." Apparently, my dad decided Mom was right because he kept his job and our travels were limited to the states around Illinois.

It had been a very long time ago, I thought as I watched Lo sleeping now. I had never thought about how tough my illness had been on my parents. No wonder my mom had developed bleeding ulcers. CF was already eating my guts out. I had been oblivious to their worries in the years following my surgery. As far as I was concerned, once the eye was gone, I was ready to go on with my life. Until now, it hadn't occurred to me that my ability to move on was because my parents had so quietly shouldered the burden of the lingering threat.

If we can only be as wise as they had been, I hoped. But the fact remained that Lo's illness was incurable. Even during the ten long years of waiting and watching for additional signs of cancer, my parents had been able to hope for the best. For Lo, each day that passed meant cystic fibrosis had inflicted more damage to her body.

"We'll do whatever we can, little woman," I reiterated my promise to Lo, gently squeezing her hand three times.

Chapter 8

TIME OUT

physically, emotionally, mentally and spiritually we were expending every ounce of energy we had. After the first five months of Lo's life I knew it was time for Terry and me to begin to search for ways to keep our marriage intact. "Sweetie, we've got to get away for a weekend," I broached the subject one evening.

"And leave the girls?" she sounded somewhat shocked. I had anticipated just such a response from my protective wife.

"I know it seems bold but we have to do it. For our sakes. If we don't spend some time together alone, we'll never make it."

"It's too soon. Who will take care of them? What babysitter will be able to do everything that has to be done with Lo and still have time enough for Jane?"

"If you leave instructions, I'm sure they can be followed. I'm not talking about a permanent leave of absence. Just a weekend." I held my ground.

"I don't know, Don. I'm still overwhelmed with all of it. In fact, I'm exhausted."

"That's exactly my point. How are you going to be able to keep up this pace for the next eighteen years without a break? We've got to take some time for ourselves. You haven't had an uninterrupted night's sleep yet."

"But when could we possibly go? Christmas is coming up . . ."

"Next weekend. This weekend. The sooner the better."

"Let me think about it."

I was making headway. "Don't think too long. I'm ready to go."

I knew Don was right although finding a babysitter for the girls was an exhaustive affair in and of itself. Several days passed before I came upon a college student who seemed to hit it off with Jane and didn't rush out the door when I explained the tasks associated with Lo's care. I made reservations at a local hotel not too far from our house. I had become pretty excited about the thought of having my husband alone for a couple of days. Then, more trouble came knocking. Two days before our holiday, a typical Oklahoma sleet storm left its slick signature on the streets. Don took my station wagon to work because it handled the ice better than his car.

Around lunchtime, he called. "Terry? I did take your car this morning, didn't I?"

"Of course you did, silly," I teased. "How can my down-to-earth, never-forgets-anything husband ask a question like that? You've obviously been around me too long."

"Yeah, that's what I was thinking," Don laughed half-heartedly. "The only problem is that your car isn't here any more. I came out to the parking lot and couldn't remember where I'd

parked it. I walked around the lot three times. Your car's gone, Terry. It's been stolen."

As it turned out, there had been a ring of car thieves working in the area. They had successfully slipped locks and jimmied ignitions in only seconds, evading notice of nearby pedestrians. The police promised to do what they could, but cautioned us that many vehicles were being found stripped, if they were found at all.

"Unbelievable," I shrugged when I finally got home that night. "You'd think we had enough going on in our lives, wouldn't you?"

"That's a very good point. Don, do you think we should cancel our weekend?" Terry asked.

"Not a chance. There's nothing we can do about the car. If they find it, they find it. I just want to put it out of my mind, along with everything else."

Terry reluctantly finished packing the next day. By late afternoon, we were loaded and ready to go. "I think it's all here," she told Debbie, our bubbly babysitter, as she handed her the voluminous list of instructions and gave each of the girls a hug.

"When will you and Daddy be home, Momma?" Jane's eyes misted as she clung to her mother.

"Sunday afternoon." Terry gently disengaged Jane's hold. We all headed through the garage to the car.

"You and Lo are going to have fun this weekend, Jane," I tried to reassure her. "Debbie, don't hesitate to call Terry's mom if you have questions. She knows what's going on. And if there's an emergency, here's the number where we'll be. But," I added hopefully, "I'm sure you won't need it."

"We'll be just fine," the astute young lady smiled. "You all have a nice time and don't worry about us. Hey Jane, let's go play a game. Okay?"

"No. I want to watch them go." Jane looked imploringly at us, no doubt hoping for a last minute invitation to come along.

"Suit yourself, Jane-O," I said. "But we'll be back before you've had time to miss us."

"I love you," Terry waved as we drove off.

"Why do I feel so guilty, Don?"

"It's universal," I told her. "You'll get over it."

It didn't take long for me to admit that Don's determination to leave had been a good idea. After a couple of hours, we were joking and conversing about subjects we hadn't had time to think about in months. I had forgotten how much fun it was to be alone with my husband. We did a little bit of Christmas shopping, enjoyed a leisurely dinner at the hotel, and had just dozed off when the phone rang. "Hello?" Don answered.

All I could hear in the background was ". . . Tulsa Police Department." My heart leaped into my throat as I envisioned disaster at our home. Had my worst fears been realized? How could we have left our little girls in the first place?

"Tonight?" Don asked, looking at me.

"What is it?" I asked, my heart pounding frantically.

Don put his hand over the receiver and whispered, "They've found the car."

"Oh, thank God!" I breathed a giant sigh of relief. My girls were safe. At that point, I could have cared less about the car.

Don listened for a few moments before saying, "I guess if that's what we need to do, that's what we'll do. What was that address again?"

After hanging up, he turned to me and frowned. "Isn't that about right? You think you can let your guard down. Then you get hit with a call from the police department!"

"At least it was about the car and not the girls," I sighed again. "What is it we have to do? You said something about tonight."

"They want us to go identify the remains. I guess they pretty well stripped it. I'm going to call Phil. I don't want you going anywhere tonight. You just stay here and go back to sleep."

For the next two hours, my law partner, Phil, and I drove around in a fairly remote area several miles north of town trying to find the address the police had given me. Addresses aren't too easy to locate in the middle of the night in a strange part of town. The car had been totally vandalized. I was glad I hadn't let Terry come with me. I figured it would have only upset her to see her car's dashboard ripped off, upholstery stained, hubcaps missing. By the time I returned to the hotel, it was nearly two o'clock in the morning. It had been my idea to get away for some rest and relaxation. After one night, I was more tired than I had been before we left. So much for our first attempt at a parental time out!

And yet, even the few hours we'd had together convinced us that spending time alone was going to be a necessary part of coping with our circumstances.

"You were right, Don," Terry admitted on our way home. "Getting away was a good idea."

"It gives us a chance to remember we're more than just caregivers," I grinned.

Terry laughed. Her laughter had been a welcome sound all weekend. "Good point. It also kind of re-energized me, even with the friendly call from the police department."

"I can promise you," I announced, knowing this was my chance to solidify another weekend, "we'll go home and be better parents. We've been under more stress than we probably even know. Unless we force ourselves to leave now and then, stress will devour us."

"You know, you're right." Terry said thoughtfully. "Until these last couple of days I had no idea how high a gear I was in. I hate to admit it but maybe we need more than a night or two."

"That can be arranged," I said eagerly.

We made plans for a second vacation two months later. This time we decided we'd get on an airplane and spend five days playing golf at a client's beautiful resort in Palm Springs. We could leave the girls in Terry's mother's capable hands, with a "back-up" babysitter. We knew Dr. Kramer was at the other end of the phone. Friends volunteered to see that Jane was transported to and from a variety of entertaining activities. Surely, this time, we thought, there could be no more emergencies to undermine our effort to keep our marriage alive.

On the day before we were to leave one of the guys on my Sunday night pick-up basketball team called. "You going to be there tonight?"

"Wouldn't miss it. There couldn't be a better way to start my vacation. Terry and I are heading to Palm Springs tomorrow for a little rest and relaxation."

"Sounds like a winner. See you at six."

Terry was busy packing as I grabbed my keys hours later. "Have fun," she yelled. "Just don't get hurt."

Famous last words. In the final game of the night, I stuck my hand out to intercept a pass. The ball caught the tip of my little finger. I knew I'd broken it before I even looked. Sure enough. The bone was sticking out the side.

The next day, instead of boarding the plane to head to California with my wife, I rode a gurney to surgery where two pins were inserted into my finger. To add insult to injury, I re-broke it a week later, when my foot slipped as I pushed my ice-stranded car. The pain of the pins bent by the blow of my hand onto the car was severe. However, it was even worse when the doctor, in the middle of trying to straighten the pins, had to retrieve the one instrument he needed from the hospital across the street. I was left lying in his office, the local anesthetic completely worn off, until his return. The rest of the procedure was completed without painkillers of any kind. The vacation we'd hoped to take was cancelled.

At that point in our journey of coping with cystic fibrosis, we could have given up. It was as if man and nature had teamed up against us. It didn't seem to matter what we said or did; disaster was always lurking around the bend. We were still reeling from the diagnosis, still stinging from having had our car stolen; I was still in physical pain. And yet, running away was never an option to either Terry or me. In a strange way, both of us were beginning to realize that one of the ways we would cope with our situation was to cling to one another for support. We knew that there was no one else in the entire world that could truly identify with all we were going through, how tired we felt, how confused we were. We had never depended upon one another more. Though it took a conscious decision on a day-to-day basis, we both continued to put one foot in front of the other, to live one minute to the next, leaning upon each other for understanding.

Chapter 9

HOPE FOR
A CURE

"*Therese, how's it going?*" Kathleen
Hilti, a childhood friend with whom
I'd stayed in contact, called to ask.

"*Well, there's never a dull moment,*" I laughed. "*I wouldn't
have envisioned myself as a nurse. Poor Lo.*"

"*I have an invitation for you and Don.*"

"*Really? To something fun?*"

"*I don't have any idea. How would you all like to go with me
to a CF support group meeting? They're going to have one tomorrow night at the medical school.*"

My aimless conversation ended abruptly. "*A support group
meeting for CF parents?*"

"*For patients, parents and interested friends.*"

"*Kath, you're too good,*" I said, touched not only by the fact
that she had discovered such a group existed but that she would
initiate our attendance together.

"Hey, you guys aren't in this alone, you know. Your friends are trying to figure out what we can do, too. Maybe it'll help to meet other people who are going through the same thing."

"Don and I have wished we could see some patients who managed to live past twenty," I said. "And we'd love to talk to their parents to see how they cope."

"Sounds like a date to me," Kathleen said enthusiastically.

"Thanks. That means so much to us. I'm sure we'd both love to go. Let me see if I can get a babysitter. I'll call you back."

The next night turned out to be a revelation for the three of us. The patients who came were typically bearing unwieldy machines that pumped oxygen into their weakened lungs. Their breathing was rapid and far too shallow. Their faces were incredibly pale, their bodies starvation thin and obviously ravaged from years of battling cystic fibrosis. Their parents looked sick as well. I speculated they were sick and tired of fighting what appeared to be a losing battle. It was a stark reminder that medical science had not made much progress. My heart went out to each of these strangers with whom we shared so much in common.

We sat through an hour of the support group meeting as one-by-one, patients and families discussed their overwhelming problems. Finally, I could stand it no longer and we left. "If this is the script of our lives, I don't want to rehearse it," I said as we made our way to the car. We were all depressed and rode in silence back to the house. Our conversation reconvened in the den.

"There's got to be something we can do," Kathleen reflected. She had watched and listened with an acute sensitivity the whole night. Suddenly, her face brightened. Little did we know the weight that her next words would carry. With no regard for the effort that might be entailed, but with total conviction, she announced, "I've got it! We've got to find a cure for this disease."

There was something powerful about the word 'cure.' It was

as if a huge spotlight had revealed a clear path where before there had been only dark shadows. "A cure for Lo," Don said. The words held a power of their own. I dared to close my eyes and capture the faint vision of such a dream.

Opening them, I looked at Don and Kathleen. We grinned in unison. There were tears in our eyes from a wellspring of hope that had not been tapped for months.

"We can raise money for research," Kathleen began. As if it would be a simple task, she offered, "We'll start a foundation." Formerly a nationally ranked junior tennis champion, she had connections to world-renowned tennis celebrities. "Maybe we should have a tennis tournament. I could call Chris Evert."

"Raising funds could give us a sense of purpose," Don added. "Frustration has been consuming every ounce of energy that cystic fibrosis hasn't. This could be a whole new way to attack the disease."

"Sounds great to me!" I laughed, hugging them both.

From that evening, we began to seek out avenues to facilitate our ideas. As we shared the concept of fundraising with our family and friends, it was obvious they were more than willing to participate. "This is what we've been looking for!" was the almost unanimous response.

We soon found out that a foundation had already been started. Zealous parents, families and friends of other CF patients around the nation had envisioned the same ideas. They had laid the groundwork for the rest of us to utilize. We also discovered that a local chapter had been organized as part of the national foundation. In February of 1985, we called to volunteer our help. The local executive director, Pauletta Henry, responded with an appreciative welcome. "We're thrilled when a family is willing to participate in the chapter's activities," she said. "Creating public awareness and enthusiasm for a disease about which so little is known has been a tremendous challenge. When a local patient is diagnosed, it helps us communicate what a dreadful disease cystic fibrosis is."

"We want to do whatever we can," I replied, still basking in the possibility that our efforts might make a difference.

"I'm going to put you in touch with the chairman of our chapter's largest fundraiser," Pauletta said. "I'm sure she'd appreciate your help with the All Sports Ball. And we'd love for you to attend our annual dinner, which is coming up next week. There, you'll get to meet the people in Tulsa who serve on our CF board."

"We'll be there," I promised.

I called the chairman of the ball, who promptly paired us with the grandmother of another recently diagnosed patient. "I'd like to invite you to co-chair the sponsorship committee with Gertrude Livingston," she offered, adding, "Gertrude's grandson is the same age as your daughter. Gertrude and her husband have been philanthropists in Tulsa for years. You'll love working with her."

Having a tangible responsibility for which to formulate goals and objectives ignited energies within us that had lain dormant far too long. Here, finally, was the rest of the answer to the question of how we would deal with Lo's illness. We would give her the very best care we could from a medical standpoint, hoping that physically, she would enjoy at least some years of relative health. At the same time, we would join forces with a strong network of people in search of a cure. We knew we were running a race against the clock, but in running we gained the hope of a victory. Not only would we be helping our little girl, but we would also be helping thousands of other patients and their families for whom hope had been diminished too long.

Chapter 10

EARLY DAYS

aving witnessed Lo waste away for her first three months, it was thrilling to watch her grow and thrive in the months following her diagnosis. She was like a magnificent rosebud as it blooms, each petal displaying yet another enchanting aspect of her delightful personality. As soon as her basic needs were met, she smiled almost constantly.

At five o'clock every morning, she woke up, eager for her first meal of the day. She ingested the various vitamin, mineral and enzyme supplements prescribed, then happily gobbled up two adult-sized servings of oatmeal, a jar of baby fruit and a bottle of formula. It was as if she was making up for the months when nutrients ran through her system, whetting her appetite but providing little sustenance.

I marveled at her ability to take medications without a complaint. The acrid Vitamin E, the pungent brown syrupy multiple vitamin, the hard spheres of pancreatic enzymes. These were *positively appetizing compared to the disgusting smelling antibi-otics that she had to take when infections set in. Normal fruity sweet liquids most children take for occasional ear infections soon gave way to nauseating aromas of rare chemical compounds reserved for equally rare germs prone to attack CF patients. And yet, Lo gurgled happily away as I dispensed each foul-smelling drop. I decided to believe that God was turning these repugnant medications into delectable sweet spoonfuls of sugar as He con-tinued to keep the promise He'd made to take care of my baby.*

It was disheartening how often Lo had to battle viruses. Bronchitis, ear infections, staphylococcus, pneumonia followed one on the heels of the next. I felt like I should set a standing appointment with Dr. Kramer. I continued to dread the drive, the walk into his office, the waiting, the exam itself. It was like living the sentence over and over again; a stark reminder of the day Lo had been diagnosed. The examination itself always lasted for more than an hour, regardless of how recently we'd just been in. However, there was no way to get around the fact that Lo had to be seen when she got sick.

"Hi, Alice." I'd greet the stout little nurse who strolled in with Lo's rapidly growing file.

"Good morning, Mrs. Detrich. How is Lauren, today?" Interestingly, the nurse would never call Lo anything but Lauren. She also referred to me formally, though there couldn't have been more than a couple of years' differences in our ages. Her formal-ity seemed strange to me, as if she wanted to distance herself from my gravely ill child and me.

After jotting down a summary of the symptoms I described, she would weigh Lo and measure her head and length. Finishing her job, she would say, "Dr. Kramer will be with you shortly." Strolling slowly back to the door, she would pull it shut on her way out. Like clockwork, the file would land with a thud in the pocket built onto the door, and the little green flag would flap against the wall, signaling to Dr. Kramer that we were ready for his entrance.

I quickly learned to appreciate that Dr. Kramer never over-booked his CF patients. He allocated twice as much time as normal for their examination and evaluation. Consequently, whenever we came in, there was rarely anyone else in the office. Alice could have simply have stuck her head around the corner, handed him the file, and said, "I'm done. Your turn." But like everything else I was discovering about this man, he did things by the book. His book. And so, we'd wait for him to slide the file right back out of the pocket, rap twice on the door and walk in.

Initially, he would ask the same questions he asked every time. What medications was I giving Lo, how often, what dosage. Then he would delve into additional details about the symptoms I had described to the nurse. He would proceed to examine Lo, listening at great length with his stethoscope to several places on her chest and back. He would measure her finger with a precision ruler, and peer carefully into her ears and nose.

Throughout the examination, I tried to think of the countless questions that had cropped up since our last visit. Were these constant infections going to continue to be so constant? Did they mean the disease was progressing? Was her weight gain adequate? Should we increase her enzymes? What did the measurements of her finger indicate? Don and I wanted to know everything we possibly could about what we should do for our baby. We needed some kind of reassurance that we were in fact giving her the best possible care. There was also a part of me that wanted to frame questions in such a way that Dr. Kramer's answers could be construed as messages of hope, nuggets of insight that might serve to light the end of our tunnel. Unfortunately, Dr. Kramer's responses often amounted to "I don't know," or "I really can't say," or "We'll certainly hope for the best." I was pressing him for information that he simply didn't have. Instead, he would adjust an antibiotic, add a medication and send us home.

It took years for us to realize how heroic his methodical efforts were. His patients are among the healthiest in the nation. His meticulous attention to detail matched his aggressive response to the vicious assaults of infections. But, nevertheless, the process of visiting his office proved to be an incredible downer for me.

While I was experiencing the frustrations of these exams, Jane was generally peeking in and out of the room, looking increasingly bored. I hated having to subject her to the process, but part of her coping with the situation of having a sister with cystic fibrosis was that she didn't want to be too far away from me. For the first half an hour or so, she would sit in Lo's examination room with us and browse through picture books or scribble with crayons on paper. After that, she would wander up and down the halls. Eventually, her patience would exhaust itself and the inquiries would begin. "How much longer, Momma?" followed by "Can we go out to lunch after this?" or "I'm bored, Momma. What can I do now?"

My toddler couldn't have known how clearly I related to her feelings, how I would have rather been anywhere but where we were. I wondered what picture of life Jane's mind was forming during these early days of Lo's illness. In some ways her mind worked far beyond her years. She asked questions about the world outside our home constantly, understood current events, that there were people who lived in places far away from her home. Yet questions about her own world, this world of sickness and medicines, came rarely. Perhaps it was because she sensed I had no better answers than Dr. Kramer had for me. To "Momma, is Lo going to die?" I could only reply, "I hope not.

We're certainly going to take good care of her, though." I reminded myself that Jane was just a toddler. As time progressed, I tried to draw out her impressions, hoping to offer a sympathetic ear or a word of comfort. I tried to offer explanations that would help her understand our situation. I felt wholly unsuccessful in my attempts. What three-year-old is going to understand the implications of having a younger sibling with a chronic disease? However, I was convinced that the situation must be frustrating for her. So, it didn't take much cajoling on her part to persuade me to reward her with some treat or other after our visits to Dr. Kramer.

Meanwhile, the early days after Lo's diagnosis were spent trying to re-define a sense of routine, a modicum of balance between crises. Each one of us was also struggling to re-define who we were, where we were headed, and how we were to relate to one another and the rest of the world.

Chapter II

ALL SPORTS BALL

*T*hough *frequent doctor visits damp-
ened our spirits, we were rapidly
getting a lift from our work with the
Cystic Fibrosis Foundation. Here we learned that money was
needed desperately to fund research on several fronts. One of
the most hopeful of these was the search for the defective gene,
a "CF gene" that was thought to be the cause of the disease.
Until this gene could be found and studied, hope for a cure was
basically at a standstill.*

*The year was 1985. At that time, the Tulsa Chapter of the
CF Foundation had one major fundraiser — the All Sports Ball,
held in October each year. This was the event to which we were
assigned as sponsorship chairmen along with Gertrude
Livingston. Our first meeting with Gertrude proved to be insight-
ful. We'd heard that she was the grandmother of a CF baby, a little boy about Lo's age. We didn't know that she was also a fire-*

She has me confused. I never owned a pair of jeans in all my life — or —

~~ball~~, who, in her seventies, still looked dynamite in gold-studded jeans, high heels and bejeweled neckline. She and her husband, Julius, had donated a fortune to various worthy causes over the years. Now, Gertrude was ready and eager to call upon those to whom she had offered support.

Don and I had no such cards to call in. Our previous civic activities had been primarily out of a sense of obligation. This was the first time either of us had been motivated by a cause to which we were deeply committed. We knew that the challenge of finding a cure was almost as imposing as the threat of the disease. And we were definitely not wealthy. But we were determined to change the outlook for cystic fibrosis research. We were about to see how contagious that determination would be.

The year before our entrance into CF fundraising, Henry and Anne Zarrow, Tulsa's most beloved philanthropists, wrote letters to several of their friends asking for donations to the All Sports ball in support of cystic fibrosis. Frank Deford, a senior writer for Sports Illustrated, had just published a book about his daughter, Alex, who died of CF. He was the ball's keynote speaker. The combination of these factors resulted in the ball's generating twenty thousand dollars, which more than doubled the previous year's proceeds.

I decided we needed to build upon his successful plan but set our sights even higher. I figured with proper planning and if we asked sufficient numbers of people, we could achieve whatever goal we set. To brainstorm, Don and I pulled out pads of paper and pencils. After spending weeks devising a plan, we were ready to coordinate the effort. Several of our friends who had offered help were now ready and willing to come through for us. Gertrude was also in complete support.

"We have established a goal of fifty thousand dollars in sponsorships," we announced at our first committee meeting of several thirty-something volunteers and Gertrude. "If we all write letters to our friends, explaining why we need their help, maybe they will join our cause. If we write to enough people, I am convinced donations will add up to fifty thousand dollars." I handed out our outline of specific ideas as to how we believed this handful of individuals was going to raise more money than had ever been raised by the local organization. We hoped that Gertrude's contacts alone would account for ten thousand dollars.

Over the summer, our committee met many times. We created lists of potential sponsors, wrote letters, and offered additional fundraising suggestions for the event's auction. The ideas spawned during these meetings created a synergy that none of us had ever experienced. Our ambitions to raise money to cure cystic fibrosis gave us courage to make contacts that we would never have otherwise considered. We were energized by the idea that we were making a difference and bound by the amazing chemistry that propels a worthy cause forward.

One morning Jane, now a self-confident four-year-old, spent several hours in her room, intently painting pictures. Upon completion, she carried an impressive stack out to the kitchen. "I'll be back in a while, Momma."

"Where are you off to, little girl?" I asked curiously.

"I am going to go to all of our neighbors' houses and sell these pictures. That's how I'm going to raise money for cystic fibrosis."

"Janie, I think that's the best and sweetest idea you've ever had," I said, my eyes welling up with tears as I surveyed the pages covered with splotches of colors.

An hour later, she was back, grinning from ear to ear. "I raised $4.38, Mom! Here, you can give this to research. It will be the first donation to the All Sports Ball."

"There will never be a better one, honey." I said proudly.

"*Thank you, Jane.*"

At the next committee meeting, Jane's creativity inspired more ideas. "*I think we need to auction off a gourmet dinner,*" suggested Don Eller. *Several of our friends were locally renowned for their cooking flair.*

"*Hey, that sounds like a great idea,*" his wife, Leah, responded.

"*We'll donate the liquor,*" Bob Stewart offered.

The initiator of the idea laughed. "*We'll all prepare different courses and serve them. At your house, Stew.*"

Mary Stewart had listened to the others' suggestions thoughtfully. "*Our table seats ten. If we prepare the dinner for five couples, they can combine their donations and we'll get more money for it.*"

By the time the plans were finalized, the dinner included a limousine service, a multi-course menu, exquisite wines, and the promise of an unforgettable night's entertainment, provided totally through the generosity of the committee. Each time word spread of the work that was being done, other generous offers came in as well. The momentum was building.

During the week of the event, we received news that convinced us our efforts were soon to be rewarded. "*Terry, are you sitting down?*" Don called at ten in the morning. I could tell his voice sounded upbeat.

"*Why? Should I be?*" I asked.

"*I just got a fax from the CF office. They've found a marker for the gene that causes CF.*"

"*Oh, my God,*" I could barely breathe.

"*It's the first major discovery research has made in decades.*" Don scanned the message he'd been sent. "*They're comparing it to finding a needle in a haystack.*"

Chills went up and down my spine. It had been a year to the

day since Lo's diagnosis. I recalled a statement Dr. Kramer had made at that time about research money being difficult to come by since so little was known about the disease.

In my state of exhilaration and naïveté, I corralled the girls, my mom, and Gertrude, picked up a copy of the fax from the CF office and headed to the local TV station just blocks away from my parent's house. We assumed everyone in the world would want to hear this incredible news. Our ecstatic faces and inside scoop convinced them that this was headliner information. The local media aired the story about this remarkable breakthrough. The timing couldn't have been better publicity for the All Sports Ball.

In addition, the contributions from the letter campaign flowed in. The response was as wonderful as we had hoped. Donations came from friends, both distant and near, current and past. By the day of the ball, we had reached our fifty thousand-dollar goal.

As we got ready for the ball on the evening of the event, Don and I were a bundle of excitement and nervous energy. We had spent the day at the fairgrounds exhibition hall decorating. "I'm scared to death I'm not going to be able to match faces and names I've known for years," Don said, pulling on his jeans and lucky number "7" football jersey. The dress was intended to be casual or sportswear, so that people would spend their dollars on contributions for research rather than formal wear. "Do you have that list of sponsors I can scan?"

"It's right here," I pulled a program out of my purse.

"Look at this. It's as if everybody we know has stepped up to the plate. A regular 'Team CF.' Kind of humbling."

I pulled Don's arm around my shoulder so I could review the list at the same time. It was truly amazing how many names we recognized as having responded to our letters. "We're not fighting this one alone. That's for sure," I said through tear-filled eyes.

We were reminded of this concept over and over throughout the night as we watched seven hundred people spend an additional twenty-five thousand dollars on auction items in a frenzy of charitable giving. No one cared that we ran out of food due to the overwhelming attendance. Laughter and tears mixed freely with music and cheers of enjoyment. Everyone was caught up in the spirit of the cause, happy to be a part of the contagious enthusiasm that had captured the community.

One friend from a childhood swimming team borrowed a dime to call his brother regarding a Caribbean cruise. He and his wife, another elementary school friend, were the high bidders. A client of Don's spent thousands. The owner of our favorite hamburger haunt won a quilt made by my mom in a raffle. "Auction it off!" he yelled, donating back his prize, creating the opportunity to raise hundreds of additional dollars through bidding. Other friends and acquaintances bid, as they were able. The ball was propelled into one of the most lucrative events in the community. It set a precedent for the future as one of Tulsa's favorite functions.

The memory of that night captured far more than an enjoyable evening for us. It solidified our decision as to how we were going to deal with our circumstances. It would be a joint effort with the help of our family, our friends, acquaintances and even strangers who adopted our cause. We began to believe that the deadly prognosis, which had walled us in for the past year, had a chink in it. Through that chink shone a bright ray of hope.

Chapter 12

SOUND OF
DEATH

Our entry into the world of cystic
fibrosis fundraising bolstered our
spirits during the sieges of infection
that continued to attack Lo. During her first two years, she
was hospitalized several times. With each hospitalization, the
number of medications she had to take increased and the regimen to which we adhered became more time-consuming.

I can still remember a conversation with the nurse who
discharged Lo after one hospital stay. "Here are the doctor's
orders," she said, handing me several sheets of paper. "The
Nystatin will help the yeast infection she has contracted from
the antibiotic. Vitamin K is another supplement kids with CF
frequently begin taking at about her age.

"I can't believe how many medicines she's on," I said
dejectedly. "Pretty soon, we're going to have to add on a stor-
age room to our house for all this stuff."

"Oh, wait till she gets a little older," the nurse laughed. "This is really nothing."

"Gee, thanks," I replied, somewhat sarcastically.

There is no way a hospitalization ever becomes routine. But, as the frequency and duration of our stays multiplied, we tried to learn from experience how to minimize their distress to our family. Terry and I continued to alternate staying one night at the hospital and one night at home. Concerned friends often delivered home-cooked meals. Visitors brought flowers and presents for Lo. Some thoughtfully included Jane on their care package list, or offered to take her on an outing. However, most of the time, even though it wasn't much fun, Jane chose to stay with us.

Memories of my own surgery prompted me to try and create ways of making Lo's hospitalizations more fun. One of our favorite activities involved me putting her in a wagon and propping her up on some pillows. Pulling the wagon with one hand and the IV pole with the other, we'd walk around the pediatric floor, waving at everybody we'd see. All the kids whose parents weren't able to be there would slowly come out of their rooms and join our parade. By the time we'd go around the floor several times, we might have a group of ten or fifteen merry pranksters singing and giggling behind us.

Eventually, we'd have to return to our room for the night. During one hospitalization I decided to institute some changes of my own. We'd settled in for an evening of great NBA basketball play-offs on TV. Lo was still quite young but I was sure she would share my enthusiasm for the luck of having something so entertaining to watch. After several minutes of listening to her dad try to explain the difference between Kareem Abdul-Jabarr and Akeem Olajuwan, for some reason, Lo lost interest. She chose instead to test the limits of her fully adjustable, conform-to-your-needs automatic bed. I, on the other hand, became increasingly aware of my own quarters for the evening. I was trying to fit my six-foot frame into a hospital crib without success.

"This ain't going to cut it another night," I announced to Terry the next day as I winced with pain. "Come on."

"What are you talking about?" Terry rushed behind me suspiciously, as I marched down the hall.

"It's ridiculous to make a grown man or woman sleep in a crib all night, for Pete's sake," I reasoned. "We've got to get some rest, too." We went on a room-by-room search through the hospital until I found a vacancy with a couch.

"We can't just play moving men — can we?" Terry asked as I started to pick up one end of the couch.

"Why not? Here, grab the other end." We hauled it down to Lo's room and then calmly asked for sheets. The aide delivered them, glancing at the additional furniture in the room.

"Didn't like the crib, huh?" she teased, adding, "I can't imagine that."

"A little tough on the joints," I smiled.

Other hospitalizations painfully revealed the stark threat of cystic fibrosis. One night Lo drifted off and I picked up a book to try and read myself to sleep. Suddenly, a sound broke through my tentative state of relaxation. I listened in sadness and shock to a young man coughing, choking, in a suffocating manner as he struggled to breathe. The coughs came without respite. I knew he was unsuccessfully trying to clear his airways to make way for even the tiniest bit of oxygen. No explanation was necessary. I recognized the sound as that of cystic fibrosis dealing a final victorious blow to another victim. It was the sound of death.

I slipped out of bed and threw on jeans and a sweatshirt. I couldn't bear to listen to someone die of this insidious disease. I hurried to the elevator and went down to the floor where coffee was served all night. For the next couple of hours I paced up and down long corridors, thinking, praying, trying to make sense of the suffering I had heard. The sound was one that would haunt me for years and cause me to catapult out of bed each time I heard Lo cough.

As much as my heart went out to the patient I had heard, I also couldn't help but hope that Lo would never suffer as much. I focused my mind on the promise I was counting on God to keep. And I continued to hope that researchers would find a cure soon. Soon enough for my little girl.

Chapter 13

WHEN IT
RAINS, IT
HAILS

The experiences that occurred between Lo's birth and her first birthday had been incredibly traumatic for Terry and me. We didn't know our misfortunes had barely begun. Even our determination to get from one day to the next became challenging in light of new circumstances that cropped up during her second year.

First, the real estate market in Tulsa crashed, rendering several investments we had made worthless. Loans to banks had to be repaid. Deferred taxes — lots of deferred taxes, had to be paid. "It's a whole lot more fulfilling to put deals together than it is to watch them bottom out," I grumbled to Terry.

This same crash caused several of my biggest clients to file for bankruptcy, which made for obvious implications in our practice. Law firms that had been around the city for decades began to close their doors.

"I've never known Tulsa to have tough economic times," Terry remarked. "I've lived here — in the oil capital of the world — my whole life. This town has always been on the way up, growing and enticing new people and businesses."

"Not right now, it's not," I shook my head. "Building has come to a screeching halt. People are walking away from millions of dollars of real estate because they can't afford to pay their mortgages."

"Are we going to be all right, Big D?"

"We've got enough to worry about right now," I answered. "We can't second guess the future." I wished this had been a time when we could have bought up the real estate deals that had gone sour. But we couldn't afford to further risk our nest egg. Lo's illness had forced us to take a more conservative investment path. We had to protect our savings for her needs.

To add insult to injury, during a devastating three-month period, nearly every member of our immediate family experienced significant health problems. First it was Terry's mother who needed foot surgery. Within days after her discharge, Terry's father underwent a heart by-pass operation. We no sooner got him home from the hospital than my dad had to have the same surgery!

We shouldn't have been surprised when Terry began experiencing almost daily migraine headaches and tenderness in her arms and back. Her doctor sent her to see a specialist. "You're undergoing a great deal of stress, aren't you?" the neurologist sympathized with her. "I'd like to prescribe an anti-depressant for you to take temporarily."

"But I'm not depressed," Terry insisted. "I'm not unhappy."

"Let me ask you this," the doctor said. "Do you find that tears are coming easier than they normally would?"

"Well, yes, I guess that's true. But let's consider what I'm crying about," Terry answered. "Everybody in my entire family is going through life-threatening crises. Wouldn't that make you cry, too?"

"I understand, Terry. But depression doesn't necessarily mean you're unhappy. It can just mean you're overloaded with distress. An anti-depressant will help your body respond more easily to these situations over which you have no control." Though she was less than enthralled with the idea of being on the medication, Terry agreed to take it. For a while.

Two weeks later, Lo went in the hospital because of a respiratory infection that I proceeded to contract as well. Shortly after her release, I was admitted and given three days worth of intravenous antibiotics.

It had gotten to the point where we wondered, almost comically, what else could go wrong. It was hard to believe that things would ever improve. On top of everything, Lo had to begin taking breathing treatments three times each and every day. Fortunately, the timing for this event couldn't have been better.

My brother, his wife and two young children had come to Tulsa on their way from Boston to the West Coast. Jeff and I had flown to my parents' house to be with them during my dad's operation. After we returned to Tulsa, his family decided to stay for a couple of weeks. Betty, Jeff's wife, suggested we initiate the additional regimen as a form of recreation, rather than a depressing drudgery. We agreed.

"Lo gets to start doing breathing treatments to help her stay healthier," I explained to the kids.

"What's a breathing treatment, Daddy?" Jane asked, peering at the strange device Betty was holding in her hand.

"Aunt Betty is holding a nebulizer that has medicine in it, Janie," I explained. "See how it's connected to this tube? The tube is attached to this little white box that is plugged into the wall. The box is called an air compressor. That's because it blows air through the tube into the medicine. The medicine and the air get mixed up and then pushed out the other end of the tube through this little mask that Lo will wear." Betty placed the mask over Lo's head and adjusted the elastic strap.

"How's that, Lo?" she asked.

"Okay," two-year-old Lo answered. "It feels funny."

"Say cheese everybody." Terry snapped a photo for the family album.

"Cheese," Lo smiled through the green plastic mask.

Typical Lo reaction, I thought. I continued my lesson. "Lo can breathe the medicine straight into her lungs because the air turns it from liquid, like water, into a mist. Then it goes straight to where it needs to be."

"The wheels of the bus go round and round, round and round, round and round," we all sang as Jeff turned the machine on. The children knew all the motions from preschool and were happy to participate. Lo's breathing treatments thus began with more fanfare and fun than dismay.

Physical therapy proved to be a bigger challenge with a process we quickly nicknamed "boomps," as we attempted to manually assist Lo in dislodging mucus from her lungs. It involved placing her in a variety of positions, many of which were rather awkward and uncomfortable. We would then cup our hands and pound on her back, shoulders and chest for several minutes at a time. Though we lay her across our laps or on pillows, the recommended sessions of twenty to thirty minutes twice a day were exhausting.

"That hurts, Daddy," she winced after being pounded in various contorted positions.

"I know, Lo, but that's what we've got to do to keep all that junk out of your lungs so you can play better," I explained, reminding myself why this procedure was worth the pain and effort. Sesame Street and Disney animated classics were indispensable aspects of our "boomps" sessions. Anything to help Lo forget that her mother, or father, or whoever else might be enlisted to help, was lovingly beating on her hour after hour.

It was on the heels of this season of health crises that an event occurred, which was the icing on the cake of bad luck. One Saturday morning around six, my alarm awoke me. I was planning to play an early round of golf. The first order of business was to head to the kitchen to turn on the coffee. I was naked and hadn't put my glasses on. As I reached the end of the hall, I noticed a flashlight darting around the walls of the kitchen. My heart almost stopped beating as I realized there was an intruder in the house.

A million thoughts blazed through my blurry mind. Foremost was the likelihood that I was going to have to fight to save my family. I was naked and nearly blind. I knew Terry had gone to the couch after feeding Lo during the night so that I wouldn't wake her when I got up. I yelled out to her that someone was in the house. As she flew over toward me, she exhibited a certain command of the English language that I didn't know she had. I shouted for her to call "911" while I prepared myself to fight. It was then that I heard the door between the kitchen and the garage shut. Relieved that the intruder had retreated to the garage, I assumed we had him temporarily cornered.

"Information?" I heard Terry shriek with dismay from the bedroom. "I thought I'd called '911,' not '411'! Can't you just transfer me? . . . No." I heard a click. On the second attempt, my wife dialed correctly.

When the police arrived, they burst into the house with guns drawn, diving behind chairs and under tables. Terry dropped the phone, rushed into Jane's room to pick her up out of bed and ran into our back bathroom to stay out of the fray. She left Lo in her crib. The police concluded that the intruder had chosen to exit the premises through the garage door. We'd left it wide open the night before! I don't know whether it was my imposing figure in the hallway or Terry's less than cordial greeting, but we were thankful the intruder had chosen not to confront us.

For months afterward, I spent many nights with one eye peering down the hallway. Of course, I have only one eye. Six months passed. One night when I had finally begun to sleep again a massive corn plant next to our bed, which had gradually been losing its balance, suddenly fell on top of me. In my half-awake state, I thought it was another intruder; only this one had a million arms. "Don, it's just the plant!" Terry yelled repeatedly before I finally realized what was happening. It should have been funny. However, in the Detrich family realm of calamity, it took years before I was able to muster even a single chuckle.

Several months later, a lovely house came up for sale a couple of miles away. It was a little larger than ours with towering oak trees, which provided year-round shade. Call it coincidental, but the timing was serendipitous. We decided to move. The decision served to help us let go of the past and look forward to what we hoped would be a brighter future, concentrating on the positive aspects of life and raising funds for cystic fibrosis.

Chapter 14

A BATTLE TOO
BIG FOR ONE

*I*n November of 1986, Lo was admitted to the hospital along with three other CF patients, all of whom were older than her. In between lab tests, intravenous therapies, and coughing spells, we were blessed with the frequent visits of family, friends and other CF fundraisers. Staff members, board members and volunteers stopped by daily to encourage us, bring Lo and sometimes Jane a gift. Flowers lined the sill and served as more reminders that we were on the minds of others.

Our support system was abundant and loving. Others were not so lucky. One of the patients admitted during Lo's stay was a young man whose parents had abandoned him. Cystic fibrosis had been too much for them to deal with on top of the other problems of life. The boy lived with his elderly grandmother in a remote country town. I'll never forget Garvin.

"Hi, what's up?" a not-so-quiet voice asked as an IV pole on wheels pushed open the heavy hospital door, illuminating the entrance of a small boy into our darkened room. It was after ten at night. Lo was fast asleep and I had finally drifted off as well. I blinked, adjusting my eyes to the light. Several feet of plastic tubing connected the boy's arm to a bag of medication hung from a white metal pole standing a foot or so taller than the child. He wore a faded T-shirt that refused to settle on both bony shoulders at once and blue jeans, in which he was fairly swimming.

In my amazement at having been awakened by this little nomad in the night, I almost forgot he'd asked me a question. "Not a whole lot," I answered, trying not to think about the fact that my precious hours of sleep had been disrupted again.

"I'm hungry."

"Is that so?" I couldn't figure out why he decided to share this information with me. We were virtually strangers. The only thing he knew about us was that Lo had CF and I was her mom. But there was something about this boy that tugged at my heart. His friendliness and candor were somehow refreshing, even in this midnight encounter. Maybe he just needed some company, I thought. "Let's go get something to eat, then," I offered. "Where do you think we could find food at this time of night?"

"Oh, they let me go down to the cafeteria whenever I want," Garvin laughed. "They just want me to eat."

"But what do you do with your IV pole?"

Garvin grinned sheepishly. "I ride it. Watch me."

I threw on my robe and followed him out into the hall where he demonstrated his prowess. It was impressive how he could handle the equipment as dexterously as if he was on a scooter, all the while managing to avoid getting tangled in the tubing that connected his arm to the machine.

Suddenly, it occurred to me that this little boy was fighting cystic fibrosis single-handedly. He had no parent spending the long, lonely nights with him, reassuring him that he'd be home soon, helping him deal with the fears and questions of living with his disease. No well-wishers brought him cards or candy or little gifts. In fact, as far as I knew, he'd had no visitors at all. From what little I had heard, his grandmother was overwhelmed by her own poor health. Providing her grandson with a roof and meals was apparently about all she could manage.

"Give me a sec to throw on some clothes," I said. "I'll be right back." Fortunately, Lo was still fast asleep and didn't even stir as I dressed. "Okay, let's eat," I smiled, re-emerging from the room.

"Hi, Garvin," greeted a tech as we rode down the elevator to the cafeteria. "You must be hungry again."

"Yeah," he grinned. "I'm starving!" Garvin wheeled his equipment directly to the snack and dessert area, selecting cake and chips.

"Let me get that for you," I picked up his tray, after paying the clerk at the register. I added teasingly, "You make me nervous enough zooming all over the place."

"I'm really used to it," Garvin laughed. There was no self-pity in his voice, no demand for sympathy from me, just a statement of truth that carried enormous implications. He glanced at the tray, then looked at me and smiled. I took it to be his way of saying thanks. He pulled a handful of enzymes out of his pocket and downed them with a swig of cola.

"So what do you do?" Garvin asked me as we sat down. He ripped open his bag of chips.

I took a sip of my drink. "I guess I'm just a mom."

"Oh," Garvin answered. He put a huge bite of cake in his mouth then grabbed another handful of chips. "Want one?"

"No thanks," I said. We sat together in comfortable silence for a minute. The cafeteria was practically empty. A maintenance crew was sweeping. A couple sat at a table in a far-off corner. "What do you do, Garvin?" I asked him.

"Go to school. Hang out at the hospital. Take care of my grandmother. She's sick sometimes."

"That's all pretty important stuff, " I said.

Garvin shrugged. "Somebody's gotta do it."

I looked at his straight brown hair, hazel eyes and the all-too-familiar pale complexion. I could hardly believe how thin this young boy was considering the volume of food he was ingesting. I grappled with my anger at a disease that could so effectively malnourish a body. A sudden coughing attack gripped Garvin. Hacking, choking, he sounded as if any minute he would vomit up the food he'd managed to get down. "You okay?" I asked.

"Oh, yeah. I do that all the time." He took a few shallow breaths, then continued eating.

I thought about his last statement. I knew it was true. I'd heard the other CF kids in the hall sound just the same. I'd heard it at home. None of them had ever known any different, I thought sadly. In a way, they were heroes, fighting valiantly for every single breath. "You're a good kid, you know that, Garvin?"

Another shrug, a shy smile. "I'm done."

As I followed Garvin back up to our rooms, I wondered what would happen to him after he left the hospital. I wondered how he could possibly care for himself at home as well as we attended to all of Lo's needs.

The next day, I asked Dr. Kramer about him.

"His situation is challenging," Dr. Kramer acknowledged. "His grandmother has a hard time caring for him. They are poor country people. She's ill, too. But she's all he has." Then he added, almost to himself, "We do what we can."

I realized the weight of his last statement. "That must be frustrating for you, too," I said.

Dr. Kramer smiled stiffly, then for a minute, closed his eyes and nodded. "Yes." I remembered the day he'd told us CF was the worst diagnosis he had to make. I had always wondered if he ever allowed himself to become attached to his patients. He seemed so gruff and businesslike. Something in his expression now suggested his exterior demeanor protected the feelings he harbored inside. "We still lose every patient," he said sadly.

I thought about Garvin and his solo battle. I wondered how many other CF children there were like him in cities and towns around the country. I wanted to take them all home and tend to their needs as I tended to Lo's. I wanted to give them all hope, to tell them we were working hard to raise money to find a cure.

Three years later, I thought to ask Dr. Kramer about Garvin and how he was doing.

"We lost him several months ago."

It was heartbreaking to know that a cure hadn't come in time for this brave little boy. His life had been so short and so full of suffering. There would be many more Garvins, we knew, before a cure for CF was found. But, having crossed his path, I became more determined to move forward on my fundraising efforts. This wasn't just about saving Lo anymore. I wanted to make a difference to another Garvin along the way.

Chapter 15

TAKING THE
HOSPITAL
HOME

*J*ust about the time we considered having our mail forwarded to the hospital address, an event marked a turning point in our ability to deal with chronic illness.

Lo had been on intravenous therapy for a week. We had resigned ourselves to the expectation of the usual three-week internment. Friends generously toted Jane to and from school, Terry and I briefly passed one another coming and going. Laundry piled up, meals were eaten in haphazard fashion, and Jane was tossed back and forth among relatives, playmates and the confines of the hospital. Our nerves were on edge, our patience had worn thin, and there appeared to be no end to this cycle of chaos.

It was Saturday morning and Terry and I were together in Lo's hospital room for once when a lady popped her head through the doorway. "Hi. May I come in?"

"Why not?" I invited in a weary voice.

"My name is Pati Richardson," the woman introduced herself cheerily. Her dark hair was cropped around her face. She drew a chair over from the corner and set it in the center of the room. It was apparent that she wasn't a member of the hospital staff, all of whom wore blue and white uniform shirts. Pati was dressed colorfully in a pair of stretch pants and tunic, over which she wore a short-sleeved pink uniform shirt. Surveying the room briefly, she announced with complete confidence, "We're going to be great friends."

Terry and I glanced at one another. We had absolutely no idea who this woman was. We were totally perplexed.

"You see," she explained, "I'm a home health care nurse. Dr. Kramer is going to let you go home today. You can continue your daughter's IVs there."

Home? Today? When we'd thought we had two more weeks of confinement? I looked around the hospital room. The gleaming silver poles bore bags of liquid soldiers, filing drop by single drop into Lo's body, beating back the staph infection and pneumonia that had caused her hospitalization in the first place. Registered nurses and aides were monitoring her day and night. A proficient technician changed the tiny catheter threaded through her wrist when too many days of medicine caused the vein to collapse. The oxygen ports built into the wall stood by in case they were needed at a moment's notice. Suddenly, the claustrophobic cubicle seemed to offer immeasurable security. Why would we want to leave, I wondered.

Pati read my mind. "Home hospital care is a new alternative to extended stays in an institutional environment. We provide home infusion equipment you can operate. It's more portable than what you have here and it's extremely easy to use."

"But what about the alarms?" Terry asked. "When they go off, the nurse comes rushing in to handle any problems. How are we going to know what to do?"

"I'll teach you everything you need to know. And," Pati smiled, "I'll be at the other end of the phone. I make house calls twenty-four hours a day."

"I don't know," I said reluctantly. "It's hard to believe we could give Lo the same care at home that we get here."

"I think you'll be surprised," Pati said. "The equipment is extremely safe and reliable. You'll love the flexibility it gives you. All the CF families do."

"And Dr. Kramer thinks this is a good idea?" Terry asked.

"I take care of most of his patients," Pati assured us. "That's how I know we're going to be friends." She rose out of her chair and walked over to Lo. "How are you today, Lauren?" she said, patting Lo's head.

"I'm great," our two-year-old answered. "How are you?"

Pati laughed. "Well, I'm fine, thank you." The two chatted briefly, and seemed to bond immediately. Squeezing Lo's hand, Pati turned to us again and continued. "I can make the arrangements with your insurance company. They're usually very receptive since our infusion care is cheaper than in-patient care."

"That would be a plus," I agreed.

"You all think about it," Pati said. "It's your decision. Dr. Kramer will be in later this morning. You can ask him about me. Let him know what you decide."

To our surprise, Dr. Kramer confirmed everything Pati had

said. For some reason, I suppose lack of confidence, the whole idea seemed too good to be true. However, we concluded that if Dr. Kramer thought we were capable, and if other CF families had been successful, we could try it as well.

We went home that afternoon. Within hours, Pati arrived carrying two huge bags overflowing with medications and supplies. "Now, don't be intimidated," she said, noting our dismay. "You stick most of this stuff in the refrigerator. I've brought enough to last for several days." I couldn't believe it wasn't enough to last a lifetime.

She explained how to flush Lo's IV with saline before giving her a treatment, then again afterwards with heparin to keep the vein open. She explained how to connect the catheter in Lo's arm to the portable infusion device she pulled out of one of the bags.

"And this little mechanism replaces the huge contraption at the hospital?" Terry said incredulously. "It's less than a foot long!"

I looked at the cartridge Pati was snapping into the device. "That doesn't look like enough medicine to me," I said. I was used to seeing bulky bags of liquid suspended from the six-foot silver poles.

"It's the same amount of antibiotic," Pati smiled. "It's just more concentrated." She whizzed through the set-up as if it were elementary. "You see, it's just like connecting the dots. You can't go wrong. But don't hesitate to call me." Sensing our uncertainty, she added, "Believe me. After a few times, it'll get easier and easier. You can do this." And she was gone.

There we were. Instead of having the entire pediatrics staff, we had each other. Don and Terry. Instead of the security of knowing we were in a hospital, we were at home. Alone.

Six hours later, it was time to see how well we could recall

Pati's instructions. Even with the aid of the notes we had scribbled, we were confused and nervous. The ends of the syringes were color-coded. They were supposed to be clues as to which syringes went with which needles. There were more color-coded connectors. The problem was trying to remember which color went to which end. We were concerned about the sterility of each little piece. We tried to remember whether we were supposed to flush with heparin first or second. Before the treatment or after? We were very worried we might do something that would hurt Lo. But somehow we managed to muddle our way through.

As the medication started infusing, we breathed a sigh of relief. "Don, I think we did it!" Terry said excitedly. "Can you believe it?"

"How about that?" We were both exhilarated. "I guess that makes us regular medical technicians." We began to see possibilities for this method of care.

Terry giggled. "I think to celebrate, I'm going to fix dinner."

"Oh, now, don't go off the deep end."

"Maybe I'll even throw a load of laundry in."

"Naw, let me do that for you," I offered magnanimously.

Jane suddenly appeared, bearing a stack of puzzles. She set them on the coffeetable and skipped over to the stack of videocassettes where we stored her favorite Disney classics. Then she bounced into the kitchen to get some juice. It was the first time in over a week she'd been able to get out of our sight and do what she wanted to do.

"Room to roam," I said. "Kids need some freedom to move around. That's tough to find in a hospital."

The clicking sound of the machine confirmed it was doing its job. I looked at Terry. We knew our thoughts were in unison. The liquid soldiers were the same ones that were at the hospital. They were simply marching to a new beat. This was not just a great idea, this home hospital care. It was going to be a lifesaver.

Chapter 16

INSURANCE
CONCERNS

" ow's it going?" Jim Morella, our insurance agent, asked as we began our luncheon meeting in his office's conference room. It was Jim's practice to schedule regular conferences with clients. Between sessions, Terry and I accumulated questions about our mounting concerns regarding insurance and for that matter, life in general. Oftentimes, our meetings with Jim gave us an opportunity to gain some perspective on where we had been and how we might need to alter our direction. His sincere concern and astute advice had proved him both a trustworthy friend and businessman.

"Oh, you know, Morella, the usual. Lo just went in the hospital. Or, no, she just got out." Pressing my fingers on my forehead, I squinted thoughtfully. "Let's see, maybe she recently had pneumonia. No, I think she's coming down with it."

"That good, huh?" A knock at the door interrupted our conversation. A young lady entered briefly to deliver trays of sandwiches and drinks.

I reached for a can of soda, popped the top and took a gulp. "It's tough to keep up with the Detrich family these days," I sighed. "Sometimes, I don't know whether to look up or duck."

"Sounds like it," Jim sympathized. "By the way, I saw our new poster child in the paper last week. Her smile would melt an iceberg."

"Thanks," I nodded. "Fundraising is a family affair at our house." I spread mustard on my turkey sandwich. "That reminds me. Thanks for heading up the CF River Run again this year."

"I'm delighted to do it. Just seeing Lo's face inspires me."

"She is a little cutie," I had to agree. "But we appreciate your willingness to be involved. It's encouraging."

"Hey, what are friends for?"

"We've sure found that out," I smiled. "Let us know how we can help with the run."

"I will. So what else is new, Don? How are the girls?"

I reflected for a minute. "If it weren't for CF, life would be great. Jane has pretty much taken charge and Lo figures how to make every day a new adventure."

"I don't doubt it," Jim smiled. "And Terry?"

"She would have been here today but she had to do something with Jane's homeroom." My lunch finished, I pushed my plate aside. "CF alone could be a full-time job for both of us. Terry's the one that's handling the insurance claims, which, by the way, are becoming a major part of the job description of CF caregiver."

"I can imagine. I've gotta say, I'm sure glad you all had an insurance policy in place before Lo was diagnosed."

"Took your expert advice, Morella," I kidded him.

"You're a wise man," he laughed. He stacked our plates and slid them to the opposite end of the conference table, then glanced at the legal pad by his side. "It's too bad Eller & Detrich wasn't eligible for group rates at the time your policy started. You'd have qualified for a much lower premium."

"Speaking of which," I interrupted, "We're getting premium increases about every quarter. At that rate, we're going to be paying more in premiums than we make in a few years, no matter how good our business is."

"Ouch," Jim winced. "That's what happens to high-risk customers. And don't ever cancel the policy, Don. Not unless you quit your job and go to work for a big corporation."

"I don't plan to. But why do you say that?"

"Anybody else would turn you down the minute they saw the words cystic fibrosis on your application," Jim said. "They don't make any money on catastrophic illnesses."

"Neither do we."

"I understand," Jim acknowledged. "Insurance companies evaluate cost-effectiveness of group policies based on how many healthy employees can absorb the claims of a few illnesses. It takes a lot of people to make up for one CF patient."

"Apparently," I agreed. "And that doesn't take into account the expenses that aren't covered. Lo has to take vitamins and minerals that her body can't properly absorb from food. The insurance company rejects thousands of dollars in claims because they're not considered prescription drugs. Then there's the million-dollar limit we have. With the amount of claims we're filing, we're going to exhaust our cap well before Lo grows up. I don't know what we'll do after that. We're saving as much as we can. But we could be wiped out in a year or two without insurance."

Jim shook his head sympathetically. "You all fall into a small group of unfortunate families, I'm afraid. You make too much money to get assistance but you don't make enough to be self-insured."

"Who does? All but the wealthiest people in the world would have a tough time keeping up."

"There is one option you can take to protect the million dollars," Jim offered. "The firm is now large enough to be on a group policy. You could be covered under a group plan as well as the one you're currently on and file your claims on it. You'd still have to retain your existing policy but because you wouldn't be filing any claims on it, you wouldn't be reducing your lifetime benefits."

"But we'd be paying premiums on both policies."

"I wish I had a less expensive suggestion," Jim said. "But look at it this way, Don. At least you don't have to cover the bulk of Lo's claims out of your own pocket. It wouldn't take long for the medical services she requires to equal the double premiums."

"Hmmmph. We may be forced to do that, I guess. At least until we decide we just can't afford the double hit, assuming the premiums keep going up."

"If you'd like to consider the option, let me know."

It didn't seem to matter how hard we worked, or how much money we made. We were not going to get ahead with CF hanging over us. I had never before understood quite so clearly what it meant to be caught in a rat race.

That night, I reiterated my conversation to Terry.

"It isn't fair, Don," she concluded. "People pay so much for insurance, thinking they're protecting themselves. Then, as soon as disaster strikes, their premiums go up, their policy doesn't cover all the costs, and they have to worry about running out of insurance."

"And money," I added. "But Jim had a good point. The longer we can milk those million dollars the better off we'll be. Who knows what we'll have to do at that point?"

We considered the possibility of desperate measures that might lie in our future. It became clear to me that Jim's suggestion to put the firm on a group policy and yet retain our existing private policy was the only means we had of prolonging that point in time when we would have to face such measures.

"Are you saying you don't think we have a choice?" Terry asked eventually.

"Nope. I don't. So much for that trip around the world we were hoping to take this summer."

"Very funny. Just one more consequence we can chalk up to cystic fibrosis, I guess."

"I'll give Jim a call in the morning."

Chapter 17

OTHER CASUALTIES

It was always the nights that were the hardest. For some reason, Lo's worst coughing spells would inevitably begin about four in the afternoon. As we pulled out of a grocery store parking lot one sunny spring day, she began to cough intermittently. At first, I dismissed the sound, but within minutes, it came more frequently. "Do you feel okay, honey?" I asked my toddler, taking advantage of a red light to peer at her. Her blue eyes looked a little glazed; her complexion was unusually pale, even for Lo. I reached over and felt her stomach. It was warmer than it should have been.

"I just have a little tickle, Mommy. I feel great." She patted my arm with her fingers.

"That's what you always say," I smiled, hoping to disguise the distress that suddenly gripped me. I pulled away from the stoplight, wondering if the staccato-like, sharp hack was a harbinger

of another infection. Experience had taught us that the 'tickle' often indicated a germ, particularly lethal to cystic fibrosis patients, was playing havoc with Lo's lungs. Pseudomonas is a common bacterium, so easily fought off by healthy individuals they don't even know a battle has occurred.

I recalled the day Dr. Kramer delivered the result of one of Lo's cultures. "It appears that pseudomonas has colonized in her lungs," he announced.

Don and I had read everything we could get our hands on about cystic fibrosis since Lo's diagnosis and were quite familiar with the impact of this statement. For us, it was an indication that the deterioration of Lo's respiratory system had begun. "Is there any hope it will go away?" I asked dejectedly.

"Of course, there's always hope," Dr. Kramer said. "But once the germ takes up residence, it's very difficult to eliminate. With aggressive treatment, we try to minimize the damage it inflicts. That's why I generally like to prescribe potent antibiotics as soon as we know an infection is present, or if the colonized germ flares up."

I hated the reality that the disease was destroying my little girl's lungs. Her original diagnosis had been prompted by her digestive problems as a newborn. We had since found out that complications of the digestive system were rarely as serious as those of the lungs.

The constancy of Lo's coughing brought me back to the present. It was anticipating what might lie ahead that triggered my concern most. In addition to damaging Lo's lungs, sieges of illness wreaked havoc on all of our lives. Infections meant weeks of illness, possible hospitalization, endless nights of fitful coughing, exhaustion and strain. Were we never going to have a break from this onslaught, I wondered. I struggled to dismiss my tired sadness as a surge of adrenaline prompted me into action. "Let's go home and see what we can do about this, Lo," I turned the corner, postponing a last-minute stop at the dry cleaners I'd hoped to make.

"I'll help you make dinner, Mommy," Lo offered soon after we arrived home.

I was busy lining up the copious array of drugs we kept on hand. "That'd be wonderful." In the midst of the din of cystic fibrosis, I had come to depend upon Lo as my helper. She was willing to take instructions, do it my way and keep smiling. Her cooperative nature fed my energy supply in an extraordinary way. "First, let's take this stuff, so it can start working. What would you like for a snack? You have to have something in your tummy when you take prednisone, you know. What can I fix you?"

"Marshmallows and cheese," Lo said with enthusiasm.

I shuddered at the combination of flavors.

"And some Ritz!"

I shook my head. "Whatever." I recalled that the same combination had appealed to Lo the last time she had encountered problems with pseudomonas. "Here, take these enzymes." I handed her four capsules which she put in her mouth all at the same time and swallowed with a drink of Gatorade. "How do you do that?" I marveled.

Lo giggled.

Following the snack, I continued doling out the rest of the regimen Dr. Kramer had recommended. The prednisone was a steroid that suppressed the immune system as well as the cough. However, it took twelve to twenty-four hours to work. I glanced at the clock as I listened to the ever-increasing rasps. Twenty-four hours seemed an eternity away.

I interrupted our medical administration to call Dr. Kramer's office and make an appointment for the next day.

"*Tomorrow morning at 11:30.*"

"*Okay, Mommy,*" Lo coughed again.

I used the appointment time as a marker of when I could expect Lo to begin to get relief. By then, the prednisone should begin to work. And it would also be a time when Dr. Kramer's experience would provide some relief for me. Taking care of Lo when she was really sick was worrisome. I didn't want to do the wrong thing. But I wanted to do enough of the right one.

"*Bottoms up,*" I said, giving her a teaspoonful of cough medicine, which I knew would be the first of two or three for the night. Dr. Kramer had cautioned me not to give Lo too much, as coughing was the only way she had to clear out her lungs. But he also warned me that excessive coughing could ultimately result in the lungs collapsing. I had learned that cystic fibrosis not only attacks its patients, it also regularly puts caregivers between a rock and a hard place. There are few decisions that don't have serious side effects or long-term risks.

"*Inhaler time,*" I said, picking up the first of three small canisters. Each one contained a broncho-dilator to open up the airways, which were inevitably inflamed and congested. Lo had to inhale the medication and then hold her breath for thirty seconds to retain as much of the drug as possible. "*Uno, dos, tres — cuatro, cinco, seis,*" I counted the thirty seconds in a singsong Spanish we had learned from Sesame Street. It was impossible for her to hold her breath as long as she needed. "*Just do it as long as you can.*" I said. Finally, I set her up with a breathing treatment in front of the television.

"*You can relax for a little while and I'll cut up the vegetables for dinner. When your treatment is done, you can help me put them all in the pan.*"

"*What are we having?*"

"*Spaghetti,*" I said. This was my easiest recipe as well as

being one of Lo's favorites. Oftentimes, when she got sick she lost
a few pounds. Dr. Kramer had encouraged us to try and keep her
weight up as a protection against sickness. Plus, I could make
spaghetti in my sleep. Whenever Lo started coughing like this, I
had trouble thinking about anything else except how else I could
help alleviate her symptoms.

"Mmmmm!" Lo approved, behind the vapor-filled mask.

While I chopped green peppers, onions and mushrooms, I
counted the seconds in between Lo's coughs. The inhalers and
medication in the breathing treatment were offering a little
respite. But, I knew, the respite would be very brief. It was going
to be a long night.

"Goody!" Lo said eagerly, twenty minutes later, dropping her
now-empty nebulizer and grabbing the step stool we had pur-
chased for cooking. She carefully deposited the ingredients into
the stockpot while I stirred. "Can I have a taste?"

"Let's wait a few more minutes," I said. "The vegetables need
to simmer for it to taste right."

"How about if I rinse these dishes?" she offered, coughing
intermittently.

"You're on," I accepted. With each cough, my muscles tensed
up. I wondered if hers did the same.

Shortly after, a flashing light caught my eye. I looked out
front through the open dining room window to see Don's car
pulling into the drive. At the same time, I saw another familiar
car pull in. I heard Don say, "Thanks, Cheryl," and watched Jane
climb out of the back seat.

"Hi, kids," I greeted the pair as they walked into the house
through the garage. Lo coughed again.

"Hi, Momma," Jane said gleefully.

I kneeled down to give her a hug. "How's my girl? I missed
you today."

"I'm okay."

"I'm so glad to see you, Janie." It was true. Whenever she was gone, the house seemed to be missing the zest that gave it a special character. Lo coughed.

"Me, too, Momma. What's for dinner?" Lo coughed again.

"Spaghetti."

Jane groaned, her mood souring. *"I don't like spaghetti. Why do we always have spaghetti?"*

Not wanting to engage in a battle of wits, I dismissed the comment and turned to Don. I was always relieved to have him nearby when Lo was sick. *"Hi babe,"* I said.

He grabbed a spoon out of the drawer to test the spaghetti sauce simmering on the stove. *"Mmmm, good."* Hearing Lo's spastic bursts he sympathized. *"Got a cough, my little woman?"*

"Got a tickle," I muttered.

"Oh. I see." He looked at me knowingly. *"I'll change my clothes and be right back."*

I looked at Jane who had slid by me and opened the refrigerator. She was staring dolefully at the contents. In spite of the physical strain I knew Lo was in, I realized her sieges were hard on Jane, too. I knew the night ahead might be tough for her, as our attention would be focused on Lo. I decided to spend a few minutes with her while I had the chance. *"Hey, Lo, why don't you go talk to Daddy?"* I suggested.

"Okay," my compliant little patient raced out of the room.

I stirred together the butter and herbs for the loaf of Italian bread I had sliced. *"Did you have fun at Abbey's?"* I asked Jane, who had proceeded to shift the contents of one shelf in the refrigerator to another.

"Uh-huh. I'm hungry, Momma. Can I have a snack?"

"Not right now. We're going to eat in a few minutes. Would you please close the frig? You're letting all the cold air out."

Jane obliged and moved to the pantry. "Mommy, I can't wait till dinner. I need something to tide me over."

"No, honey. It's too soon till we eat. You'll just have to wait." Hoping to get her mind off of her hunger, I asked, "What did you and Abbey do?"

"We played in the attic."

"Oooh," I said, setting the bread on a piece of aluminum foil, sliding it into the oven. "You love to do that."

"Momma," Jane said suddenly. "Can I paint?"

"Not now. We're almost ready to eat." I could hear Lo coughing in the back of the house. I could feel my muscles tighten again, responding to the sound.

"What about after dinner?"

"Honey, it's too late to paint," I said, wishing she would quit making demands I'd have to refuse. "It's time to finish making dinner. Would you like to help me?"

"No. I'd like to paint."

"Well, that's not an option, Jane," I said, feeling my patience wane. "Maybe tomorrow. I can't handle the mess right now. It's dinnertime."

"Can we go for a bike ride after dinner?" Jane, her voice still hopeful, tried a different avenue.

"Not tonight, Jane." Couldn't she hear the incessant hacking in the background? Couldn't she sense the strain that it was putting on me? Visions of Lo's body shaking from head to toe leapt into my mind.

"Why not, Momma?"

"It sounds kind of like it's going to be a long night." The constancy of Lo's cough sent adrenaline rushing through my system, like a small jolt of electricity. The tiny shock waves were having a cumulative effect, setting my nerves on edge. My reserve of patience was gone.

Jane whimpered. "Could we do something fun?"

"You can set the table." My tone of voice left no room for question. I tried to remind myself that Jane was only six, and that spaghetti was one of her least favorite meals. I wondered if our situation had been more normal, without the threat of cystic fibrosis hanging over our heads, whether I would have had more patience. On the other hand, I reasoned that the extraordinary circumstances dictated we all stretch the limits of our capacity, regardless of age. Jane would just have to learn.

"Okay, okay," she grumbled. She grabbed a handful of tableware and napkins and arranged them haphazardly around the kitchen table. "I'm going to go around the block," she announced, walking towards the back door.

"What are you thinking about, Jane?" I was sure she had seen me take the dinner plates out of the cabinet. I was already in the process of serving. "It's dinnertime. That's why I had you set the table. Why do you have to be so difficult when I'm already tired and worried? Can't you hear the coughing? Don't you know how hard it is to listen to that?"

"What did I do, Momma?" Jane asked, looking convincingly perplexed and exceedingly hurt.

I desperately needed her cooperation. I was a bundle of nerves. When was Jane going to figure out that during Lo's coughing fits, her demands would inevitably be met with exasperation?

In the midst of dealing with the onslaught of Lo's chronic disease, there were too many misunderstandings between Jane and me, leaving countless bruises in their wake. Through no more fault of her own than having been an active child with universal needs, Jane had to endure the brunt of my tension. Her level of activity became a direct reflection of my own sense of distress. At the same time, through her eyes, I should have been the one offering consolation. My attempts to separate her actions from my distress were wholly unsuccessful.

"Just go tell Daddy dinner's ready," I said irritably.

Without leaving my side, she yelled. "DINNER!"

"Jane! What was it about 'go tell' you didn't understand? I could have screamed for them to come myself. Can't you be just a little bit cooperative for once?" I could feel my blood pressure rising. I had lost my temper. "Go to your room till I tell you to come out, young lady!"

Jane immediately burst into tears and ran out of the room. Seconds later, I heard her door slam shut.

How typical, I thought bitterly, hearing Jane crying furiously. I was so confused. What had just happened? All I had wanted to do was spend a few minutes with my daughter enjoying a little conversation. I wanted to let her know that even though Lo required so much of my attention, I still loved Jane dearly. I wanted to tell her not a day went by that I didn't wish her life could be free of her sister's disease. But as always seemed to happen when Lo was sick, my desire to comfort my oldest child was preempted, resulting in feelings of hurt and pain and frustration. In many senses, the disease brought out the worst in both of us.

Chapter 18

DRUG
OVERDOSE

*T*he amount of prescription drugs and supplemental vitamins and minerals that Lo took precipitated our keeping an impressive inventory on hand. Multiple shelves in our kitchen cabinets and pantry were filled with pills, drops, broncho-dilator canisters, and equipment. The time it took to order, stock, organize, dole out and consume this pharmaceutical arsenal was staggering.

At least once a week, I re-evaluated our supply. It was unwise to order too far in advance because her medications were constantly being changed. Doses were given out three to six times a day, depending upon the delivery system used. In the morning for breakfast there were pills to take. Prior to breathing treatments, Lo inhaled a dozen or so puffs of broncho-dilators and steroid inhalers. Different liquid medications were mixed and dispensed into nebulizers for the various breathing treatments. At times, we had to use at least two kinds of breathing treatment machines. All the machines required scrupulous care to reduce the risk of contamination.

Any ideas that could streamline our efforts were welcomed. We tried not to let CF dominate our existence. Lo played her part in facilitating our schedule as much as she could. She had learned to swallow pills by the time she was two years old. By the time she was four, she could swallow several at a time. One afternoon, however, her attempt to facilitate the process taught us a lifelong lesson about the dangers of drugs.

Having completed her physical therapy session, I poured the two medications prescribed into the nebulizer for the third of four breathing treatments she was to have that day. I set Lo up in her usual spot with the treatment machine, coloring book, crayons and remote control for the TV. Each treatment lasted about twenty-five minutes. "Okay, baby," I said. "I think you're set."

"Thanks, Mommy," Lo smiled as she surfed through the channels.

I went back into the kitchen to think about what to cook for dinner. Not more than three minutes later, Lo ran into the kitchen. "I'm done, Mommy! Isn't that good?"

"How in the world could you be finished, Lo? It's only been a few minutes."

"Well," Lo said proudly, holding up the empty nebulizer chamber, "I thought it might go faster if I just drank the medicine."

"You drank it?" I said incredulously as I rushed to the phone to call Dr. Kramer.

"Yeah, Mommy, I thought that would make you happy," Lo looked puzzled.

"Marie, I need to talk to Dr. Kramer right away," I told the receptionist who answered the phone. "Lo just drank her *aerosolized medicine."*

A minute later, he was on the line. *"Check her heart rate."* he said calmly.

It had soared to two hundred beats per minute.

"That's the albuterol," he explained. *"Do you have any syrup of Ipecac on hand?"*

"No," I said, berating myself for being so stupid. Here we lived in a veritable drug store and I hadn't thought to supply our house with the most common poison antidote on the market.

"Don't panic," Dr. Kramer consoled me. *"She'll be okay. Just go to the nearest pharmacy and ask for some Ipecac. Don't wait till you get home to give it to her. Call if you need me."*

Hanging up the phone, I reached around the corner and grabbed the car keys. *"Come on Lo, let's go. Now!"* I tried not to panic.

"What's wrong, Mommy?" she said, a worried look on her face.

"We need to run to the store, little lady. We need to get some medicine real quick."

I flipped on my emergency flashers and raced down the street as fast as I dared, all the while continuing to chastise myself for failing to have the medications we needed on hand. *"Thousands of dollars of drugs in our house, child-proof locks on cabinets and drawers. But no simple poison control,"* I muttered to myself. I tried to let Dr. Kramer's comforting words that Lo would be okay ring through my concerns.

Fortunately, the drug store was only a couple of miles from our house. A parking space was available at the door. I picked up Lo and carried her back to the pharmacy counter. *"Lisa, can you help us?"* I pleaded with the pharmacist.

"What's the matter, Terry?"

"Lo drank her Albuterol. I didn't have any syrup of Ipecac to

give her."

"I see. Well, we have plenty of that," Lisa said, lifting the shelf which served as a gate between the pharmacist's dispensary and the public. "It's right over here." She hurried over to an aisle against the wall and scanned the shelves. "There you go," she spotted the bottle we needed. "Why don't you drink this right now, Lo? It's on the house," she said tearing the packaging off.

I was thankful Dr. Kramer had been in his office — thankful for the trusting relationship we had developed with the pharmacist — thankful for the cooperation of my child. And, I was relieved she was able to down the medicine without complaint. "Now what, Lisa?" I asked, again checking Lo's heart rate. It was still two hundred.

"I think you have about enough time to get home before this stuff takes effect," she said.

"Gotcha. Let's go, Lo." I carried her back to the car and rushed home. Soon after we arrived, she turned very pale.

"I don't feel so good, Mommy."

We hurried to the bathroom. I felt horrible and relieved at the same time as the Ipecac worked to eliminate the overdose from her system.

Within an hour, her heart rate had come down significantly. I knew we were out of the woods. "Hey, Lo, you know that medicine you drank?" I said as I hugged my little girl tightly.

"Yeah."

"Don't drink it again."

Chapter 19

A SECOND
OPINION

*I*n the spring of 1987, publicity surrounding our fundraising efforts helped produce
a windfall donation of thirty thousand dollars for the foundation. Everyone who knew us had also come to know of our commitment to cystic fibrosis, creating a permanent association of
our family with the CF Foundation. Consequently, when an
elderly woman of means needed to make a hefty donation in
order to realize some tax benefits, our accountant thought of
suggesting the CF Foundation as a benefactor. At the same
time, we helped a group of individuals identify, request and
obtain a major grant from another local group.

Unfortunately, record-breaking fundraising efforts did not
parallel robust health for Lo. As we pondered daily what stones
we could still overturn to help our child, a newly promoted executive director named Christy Burwell alerted the leaders of the

national foundation that a little girl in Tulsa, Oklahoma had captured the hearts of the city and that her battle with CF had been particularly tough.

One afternoon, the telephone rang. "Hello?" I answered, half distracted by Jane's efforts to roller skate through the living room.

"Mrs. Detrich, this is Bob Beall of the Cystic Fibrosis Foundation."

My attention was instantly focused on the other end of the phone. Why in the world would the director of medical affairs for the national CF Foundation be calling me? "Why, yes. What can I do for you?"

"I understand your little girl has been having a pretty difficult time with cystic fibrosis."

"Yes, that's true."

"I don't know what your situation is but I wondered if there were any way for you to take Lauren to see another doctor."

The thought of getting a second opinion had certainly occurred many times to Don and me. "If there is a reason we should take our child to another doctor, you can bet we'll be on the next plane," I said definitively.

Well, you know we have utmost confidence in John Kramer," Dr. Beall continued, "but sometimes it helps to have two heads. The treatment of patients is rather subjective. Having another physician validate your daughter's treatment might relieve some concerns."

"Who would you recommend?" Other than Dr. Kramer, Don and I had no idea where to begin to search for another CF specialist.

"We have many fine CF doctors, so don't take this as an exclusive recommendation. However, if I had a daughter Lauren's age and she had been as sick as your little girl, there are three or four doctors in the United States I would hope to run across. One *of them lives in Tucson. His name is Lynn Taussig. Would it be possible for you to take Lauren to see him?"*

I knew Don would be in full support of the idea. "I don't think that would be a problem at all," I said.

"I can make a few phone calls for you to arrange an appointment," Dr. Beall offered.

"I can't thank you enough. Of course I'll have to talk to my husband but I'm sure he'll agree." I said. "We've been wondering about this very thing."

"It's my pleasure. We appreciate your fundraising efforts on behalf of the foundation as well. We'll be in touch."

Within a couple of days, arrangements had been made and appointments set. As Jane only had a few days left of kindergarten, Don and I decided she could come along with Lo and me. The idea of getting to ride in an airplane overshadowed the potential boredom of sitting for hours in a hospital waiting room.

"Do you think you can handle the girls and all this paraphernalia?" Don asked as he loaded machines and suitcases into the car.

"I can do it." I said confidently. "We'll be just fine." I knew he was questioning his decision not to come. He was always trying to balance his professional and personal life. Demands at the office dictated he not make this trip.

After a six-hour plane delay and re-routing of our trip through Denver, Colorado, we arrived in Tucson at dusk as a rainstorm pelted the streets of the drought-stricken city. "This is fun, Momma!" laughed Jane, skipping through puddles and wielding as much of our gear as I dared to let her carry.

"Watch the cars, Jane!" I cautioned, bleary-eyed. The blisters on my feet rubbed mercilessly against my shoes. I was sure that I had carried our suitcases a hundred miles; my shoulders and elbows ached from the strain of the weight. Lo hung on to my

neck calmly as I limped cautiously up the sidewalk towards our lodging. For an instant I did question the wisdom of sauntering off a thousand miles from home for a doctor appointment.

But after a night's sleep, I awoke, refreshed and eager. I wondered how many changes, if any, Dr. Taussig would make to Dr. Kramer's orders. I couldn't help but feel a little anxious as I recalled the first time I had met Dr. Kramer. The heartache, the sudden onset of a tension headache, and nervous butterflies fought to take control as we walked up the hospital ramp, situated across the street from where we'd stayed the night before.

I looked around at the sea of strangers in the lobby. Most were of Mexican descent. From the bits and pieces of conversation I heard only Spanish. Many faces looked sad, confused, tired. I wondered if any of them looked at me and saw the same expression. Had cystic fibrosis left its mark on my posture yet? I hoped not.

"Momma, you don't have to hold my hand so tight," Jane complained.

"Sorry," I said, loosening my grip only slightly. "I just don't want to lose you." I asked the woman in the admissions window for directions to the CF Clinic.

She smiled at Jane and Lo as she answered. "Yes, dear. See those double gray doors over there? Go through them, turn left and walk almost to the end of the building. The clinic is called St. Luke's. It will be on your right."

"Thanks so much." I said. I wondered what problems all these people were experiencing. I wondered if their hearts raced with anxiety as mine was doing. Burying my feelings, I tried to talk to the girls. "We're almost there."

"Will Lo have to stay in this hospital tonight?" Jane asked.

"I don't know," I said. "We'll just have to wait and see." Don and I had decided we would be willing to consider whatever Dr.

Taussig recommended.

"You go and stay as long as you need to," Don had insisted. "Lo deserves the best care we can find. I'll support you however I can." I felt bad that he couldn't be here to listen and watch and learn but I was grateful for his commitment to Lo and his respect for my judgment.

Finally, we saw a sign that said 'The St. Luke Clinic.'

"This is it," I steered my girls toward another reception window.

"Hello. My name is Terry Detrich and I've brought my daughter, Lo, to see Dr. Taussig."

The lady flipped through some files on her desk. "Lauren Detrich?"

I smiled. "Oh, yes. Sorry. We call her Lo."

"All the way from Oklahoma, I see. Did you have a good trip?" Her friendly demeanor immediately put me at ease.

"It was eventful," I laughed, mentally picturing our journey the day before. "Let's just say we're glad to be here."

"Traveling with little ones can be a challenge," the woman commented sympathetically. "If you wouldn't mind waiting for a few minutes, we'll notify Dr. Taussig you're here."

"Thanks."

Jane and Lo walked around the waiting room curiously. A television in one corner was tuned into Sesame Street. Stacks of children's books and magazines for parents dominated end tables. The walls were of a warm, Arizona red brick. Wooden trim pieces contrasted with the red but gave a cozy, friendly feel to the room. Southwestern décor hung on the walls and accented the chairs. "I like this place, Mommy," Lo decided immediately.

"Me too," Jane agreed.

"Well, isn't that wonderful," I laughed, relieved.

"Lauren?" A nurse stuck her head through the door of the

clinic examining room area, prompting us to jump up and head her way.

After weighing Lo, measuring her height, blood pressure, temperature, pulse rate, oxygenation, and listening to her heart, the nurse ushered us into a private room, where she took a lengthy history of Lo's case. "I'll take this information to Dr. Taussig. He'll spend a few minutes reviewing it and then come in to consult with you."

"We'll be here," I smiled, hoping we wouldn't have to wait too much longer.

Several minutes later, there was a knock on the door. "Good morning!" a jovial voice greeted us. A middle-aged man with curly gray hair and kind eyes whose twinkle matched his voice entered the room.

"Dr. Taussig," I shook his extended hand. "I'm Terry Detrich. This is my older daughter, Jane," I glanced over her way.

"Jane, I'm pleased to meet you," Dr. Taussig shook her hand as well.

Jane grinned at the doctor's attention.

"And this is Lo."

"Hi!" Lo, too, extended her hand, as if picking up on the routine that had been established.

"Hello there, young lady. You've come a long way to be here."

"We're from Oklahoma," Jane chimed back in.

"Yes, that's what I hear. I've never been there but I understand it's a great place." Bowing magnanimously toward Jane, Dr. Taussig asked graciously, "Do you mind if I take a look at your little sister?"

Jane giggled delightedly. "Okay."

Dr. Taussig then picked Lo up off of the examining table and set her on his lap. With both of my children smiling, my anxiety level melted. He asked questions about our family, Lo's infections, hospitalizations, and growth rate. In between he listened to her chest, looked in her eyes, ears, nose and throat. He tapped his fingers on her stomach, tested her reflexes and studied the ends of her fingers. All the while, he managed to include comments to Jane, smiles at Lo and encouraging words to me. He shared his experiences with CF research and his hopes for the future. "It's more encouraging than ever before for these kids," he smiled. "In fact, one of our kids is a fifty-four year old grandmother." As if reading my mind, he added, "She's doing beautifully."

After his examination, he finished making notes on his report. "I'd like to run some tests, if you all are able to stay an extra day."

"We can stay as long as you think we need to."

"We can do everything this afternoon, if I can get the scheduling nurse to find us an opening or two. I'd like to have a clearer picture of Lauren's pulmonary function levels. There's a test we can run that will enable us to take some informative measurements. Normally it's difficult to do with a child this young, but I think we've got a real trooper here. Am I right?"

Lo grinned as if she recognized the compliment.

"She's very cooperative," I nodded.

"We'll sedate her a bit, do some analysis, give her some medication so she won't be uncomfortable, and then do some additional analysis. Then we'll run her through another battery of tests. Tomorrow morning I'll review the results with you and give you my impressions of any changes I'd recommend to Dr. Kramer."

"Sounds great to me," I said.

The rest of the day, we were led into laboratories, and rooms with huge pieces of odd-looking equipment. At each place, Lo was asked to breathe in and out, to blow as hard and long as she could. Because she slept through the test for which she'd been given a sedative, Jane and I left her side long enough to watch the bells and curves of the computer screens as they traced the movement of air through Lo's lungs. Shelley, the technician who supervised all the tests, explained each one to us carefully and thoroughly. "That's it for today," she finally said at five in the afternoon. "I'm sure Dr. Taussig wants to meet with you again to go over the findings."

"He said to come back tomorrow morning."

"I'll have them ready," she promised, showing us to the door.

We stopped at a restaurant to eat dinner on our walk back to the hotel. "That wasn't so bad, was it girls?" I asked.

"I wish we could go swimming, Momma," Jane answered wistfully. "I thought it was supposed to be hot in Tucson."

"I thought so too," I sighed. The clouds had persisted through the day and a chilly wind blew. "It'll be summer in a few days at home."

"Do we have to go back to the hospital tomorrow? Can we go home now?"

I shook my head. "I don't know when we'll go home, Jane. It depends on what Dr. Taussig says tomorrow." I had no idea what the tests would prompt. I wondered how much longer Jane's patience was going to hold up. I couldn't help but hope that the doctor wouldn't want to hospitalize Lo out here. She didn't seem to have any particular acute infection but I'd heard of CF patients being hospitalized periodically for "tune-ups" and wondered if he thought she was in need of one.

"Can we have some ice cream, Momma?" Jane pleaded as if asking for a concession.

I looked at my eldest daughter with weary eyes. I had been so proud of her for these last couple of days. The long flight, the waiting, the battery of tests focused on Lo all day had to have been boring. "Okay, Jane," I said. "But after that, we need to go back and get ready for bed. I'm tired."

Thankfully, the next day we were re-energized. The skies had cleared overnight, enabling the desert sun to highlight the mountains surrounding the city. We strolled back to the hospital, feeling a little less strange as we made our way through the lobby, down the corridor to the clinic.

"Hello again!" Dr. Taussig greeted us cheerfully as he entered the examining room to which we'd been led. "And how are these lovely young ladies today?"

The girls giggled in unison.

"They're happy the sun is out," I said.

"You know," he laughed, "we celebrate rain out here in the desert. It's not something we see often." Pulling a pair of glasses out of his pocket, he slipped them on and scanned the file containing the test results. Then he turned a chair around backwards and sat down leaning his arms on its back. "First of all, there's almost nothing I would change in Lo's routine. I think Dr. Kramer is doing a wonderful job."

"That's good to know," I said truthfully. This confirmation certainly boosted my confidence in all the medications Dr. Kramer had put her on.

"Secondly, I would tell you that you are doing a great job, too. It's obvious from your children's behavior that they are developing normally, that you are asserting discipline, teaching them well, in addition to following the rigorous demands of a CF parent. My hat's off to you and your husband."

"Well, thank you," I was taken aback. I hadn't realized how good it would feel to have the vote of confidence from a doctor who would have an idea of the commitment necessary to care for a child with cystic fibrosis. In spite of our efforts to be good parents and caregivers, Lo had continued to be sick and we worried about how much Jane had suffered from the impact of the situation. *"That means more than you know."* I swallowed hard.

"The tests show that Lauren's pulmonary functions are still close to normal."

"Thank God," I smiled, relieved. *"Does that mean she doesn't need a tune-up?"*

"Exactly." He turned to Lo.

"Do you take dancing, Lauren?"

"I take gymnastics."

"Terrific! What do you like best?"

"I like to jump on the trampoline."

"Great. Do you do it every day?"

"Almost. We have a trampoline in our back yard."

Dr. Taussig looked at me seriously. *"I cannot emphasize how important it is for her to remain as active as possible. The very best advice I can give you is to push this little girl to follow her dreams. If she wants to be in the Olympics, there is no reason for you to discourage her. I have no desire to play God, to make predictions either way. But medical research is moving forward. Some day we're going to find a cure for this disease. Till then, we want Lauren to stay in shape so she can take advantage of new medicines."*

I knew Dr. Taussig couldn't guarantee that Lo would survive long enough to be cured. But he said enough to help me believe the effort was worth the try. Fundraising had given us hope of creating opportunities for research. Dr. Taussig's encouraging remarks gave us hope to continue the battle at home as well. His simple message had made our trip more than worthwhile, as it continued to ring in our ears whenever battles with cystic fibrosis ensued.

Chapter 20

JUST TRUST ME

One Saturday morning Lo skipped around the corner of the hall into the den where I lay on the floor stretching.

"Hi, Daddy." The sound of that sweet little voice was always welcome.

"Hi. What's up, Lo?" I pulled one leg as close to my chest as it would go, noting the vast distance between the two, and counted painfully to ten. Lo watched carefully and then plopped down beside me.

"Is this how you do it, Daddy?" she said, bending her leg and easily laying it against her torso.

"Yeah, Lo, that's how you do it," I said, marveling at the flexibility of youth. For the next few minutes we worked in relative silence, save the grunts of the father, continuing various stretching calisthenics. "That's it for me," I sat up, relieved it was over.

Lo popped up onto her feet and waited for me to do the

same. "Daddy, can we ride bikes?" Her eyes were shining and expectant. As she stood there waiting for my answer, I couldn't help but smile. This little girl has so much spunk, I thought. In spite of her illness, she had energy and enthusiasm to burn. I couldn't resist.

"Well, I suppose we can do that." I agreed. So much for the run I was getting ready to go on.

"Goody!" Lo wrapped her arms around my neck and pulled my face to hers. "Now, Daddy?"

What could I say? She had me in the palm of her hand. "I guess this is as good a time as any." Then I had a sudden brainstorm. "Hey, Lo, you think you're ready to take those training wheels off, yet?"

"Absolutely not," said Terry, who was walking through the family room carrying a load of laundry. "She's only four years old, Don. What are you thinking?"

"I'm thinking you're a mom," I teased her.

Terry lowered her chin, raised an eyebrow and glared at me accusingly. She shook her head. "It's useless," she said.

Lo looked at Terry for a second as if assessing the situation. Obviously, Mommy's stance on the matter was not as strong as she was trying to make it sound. Behind the glare, there was a little twinkle that told Lo she would rise to the challenge. Even at four, Lo was a diplomat. Recognizing her mother's statement as one that left the door open to my suggestion, she looked at me and asked very seriously, "Do you think I can do it, Daddy?"

"Sure I do." I answered confidently. "I know you can do it, Lo. Just trust me."

"Okay," she said. If her dad said she could, then she could. How much easier life would be if children could retain this attitude forever, I thought.

"Don't you just love this kid?" I grinned at Terry.

"Yes, I love her," Terry smiled at Lo. "But I think you are out of control."

"Come on out and watch us."

"I wouldn't miss it for the world," she said, toting her load back to the bedroom area. "In case I have to pick up the pieces."

"There'll be no need for that," I promised. "Get your jacket on, Lo. I'll meet you on the driveway." I headed to the garage, wheeled the little bicycle outside and proceeded to remove the training wheels, which I believed had served their purpose.

"I'm ready, Daddy." Lo scampered down to the end of the front porch, zipping up her jacket. I knew she was eager to test her skills.

Positioning the bike on the street in front of our house, I motioned to Lo. "Okay, here's the deal. You put your feet on the pedals and stand up on the bike while I steady it. At first, I'll hold onto the seat and guide it. Then I want you to start pedaling as fast as you can. Once you're going fast enough, the momentum will keep you from falling. I'll run along beside you and if anything goes wrong, I'll be there to catch you. Got that?"

Lo looked at the bicycle, leaning on its kickstand. No longer did the training wheels offer the security that had always been there. She looked up at me. I knew she was looking to see if my expression held the conviction of my words. It was my word against the training wheels. "I got it," she said.

Suddenly I realized that my daughter was about to risk her physical well-being strictly on the basis of her faith in me. It was a determining moment that I would hold onto dearly. I wasn't about to let anything shatter that trust.

"Okay. Now, stand on the pedals." Lo grabbed the handle bar and pulled herself up. I steadied the seat with one hand and the handlebars with the other. "Ready?"

Lo's eyes were focused on the road ahead. "Ready."

"Start pedaling. I've got you." Her right foot pressed down hard, then her left foot. As the bike gathered momentum, I encouraged her, "That's it, Lo. Keep pedaling."

With utmost confidence, she followed my directions explicitly. I began to run to maintain my position. After a few more seconds, I let the seat go. "You're doing it, Lo. You're on your own!" Down the street we went, Lo dutifully pedaling with me racing alongside. We were almost at the end of the block when she began to lose control. The handlebars started to wobble, the front tire aimed directly at the curb. I knew the next few seconds would test Lo's ultimate faith in me. The wheel crashed into cement and Lo flew over the handlebars. I leapt into the air to catch her and to make sure I was the one who hit the ground first. As we went down I could hear the bicycle sail over our heads and land in the grass. For an instant, we lay on the ground in silence. I knew I had caught Lo and I was sure she was physically okay. But I wasn't so sure how she was going to feel about the crash landing.

"We did it, Daddy! We did it!" Lo started laughing. How like Lo to give me half the credit for her achievement. Her eyes shone brighter than ever, with the confident air of victory. As I pulled myself up again, I barely noticed the aches and pains in my body. Together we had proven the immeasurable value of trust, and that was the only thing that mattered.

Chapter 21

GENE
DISCOVERY

Our fundraising efforts made us feel like we were on the front lines of the war against CF. We had progressed from the dismal outlook we'd been given at the outset, to the anticipation of the day when the actual gene that caused cystic fibrosis would be found, convinced that the discovery of the genetic marker had greatly accelerated the search. In the meantime, we celebrated each breakthrough, no matter how small.

By the time Lo was five years old, we felt as though we were playing a high stakes game of "Beat the Clock." Would we raise enough money to fund the research that was needed? How soon would the gene be located? How soon after the gene was found would we have a cure? And always the question boiled down to the issue that weighed most heavily on our minds. Would it be in time for Lo?

On August 23, 1989, my secretary came into the office. "Don, I think you might want to read this fax that just came. It's from the CF Foundation."

My heart skipped a beat as I stared at the document she handed me. "I sure do," I said. "Thanks." I knew that foundation faxes indicated something special, something that couldn't wait for phone calls or board meetings to relay. In fact, I had only received three or four faxes since our work with the foundation had begun. Terry and I had been talking about the fact that we hoped another one would come soon.

I sat for a minute before flipping the cover sheet. Then I turned it over and read:

'Foundation-supported scientists at the Hospital for Sick Children, Toronto, Canada, and the Howard Hughes Medical Center at the University of Michigan, have announced the discovery of the location of the gene that causes cystic fibrosis.'

Still focusing on the paper that lay in front of me, I automatically reached over and grabbed my phone. "Terry," I said a moment later, my voice husky with emotion. "You want some good news?"

"Sure," she said. "Always."

"They found the gene."

Silence on the other end was followed by a tearful shout of joy.

"Pretty amazing, huh?" I said.

"It's a miracle, Don."

I took a deep breath. In a fleeting second, a thousand visions raced through my mind. Memories indelibly etched by experience. Lo, as an infant, a toddler, and now a little girl — coughing her guts out, shaking from head to toe; Terry, tiptoeing out of our bedroom in an endless series of midnight crises to take care of Lo; Jane, looking on in a kind of confused loneliness, as our focus on Lo became the constant in our family. Was this life we had grown to live going to have a happy ending after all? "Gene therapy," I said.

"What?"

"Gene therapy. That's the next step."

"For research, you mean."

"Yeah."

"I'll bet that's going to be expensive."

"No doubt. But you know what?"

"I think you're right," Terry read my mind. "We just might do it."

"Give my little girls a hug for me," I said.

I hung up the phone, leaned my chair back and put my feet on the desk, not to relax, but to reflect on the series of events that had led to this morning's announcement. I re-read the fax. A quote from Frances Collins, one of the scientists credited with the discovery, jumped out at me.

'From encouraging collaboration, sponsoring meetings and putting dollars into the whole effort, the Cystic Fibrosis Foundation's role has been critical. We wouldn't be talking about this discovery today if the Foundation had not been involved.'

It was so rewarding, I thought, to be associated with an organization that took destiny into its own hands. For that is what had really happened. In the four years since the genetic marker had been discovered, the motto of the foundation had been that we were going to buy the science that was needed.

Finding the gene was the result of enlightened leadership, incredibly dedicated scientists, technology and yes — I smiled, a vast army of creative and committed fundraisers. Terry and I, our family and friends could be proud of the fact that we had played a part in the search through six billion base pairs that make up our genes to find the one that caused cystic fibrosis. It had taken in excess of $60 million but we had done it. We had helped raise the funds that had enabled researchers to identify this single elusive piece of DNA — 250,000 base pairs long. The scientists, fueled on by All Sports Balls and other similar events around the United States, had discovered that three missing base pairs caused the gene to create a defective protein that resulted in cystic fibrosis. Together, we had found the three in six billion.

The announcement was clearly the most exciting finding in the thirty-five years of the foundation's history. Suddenly, we had the critical tool needed for unraveling the mysteries of the disease. We knew once the basic defect was understood, new therapies and controls could be developed, namely gene therapy.

I knew the celebration would be a short one. We didn't have time. We were still playing "Beat the Clock." We would have to push ahead with more determination than ever. The Reagan/Bush Administration had curtailed billions of dollars in funding for our partner, the National Institute of Health. The responsibility for funding research, the need for public awareness of the disease and its impact on patients and families was resting squarely on our shoulders. But a milestone had been reached. I savored the moment.

The announcement was fortuitous for another reason. It provided an answer of hope to a question we knew was inevitable.

Steve Owens, the former Heisman Trophy winner and All-American running back from the University of Oklahoma, was promoting a golf tournament benefiting CF at the time the gene was discovered. While playing for the Detroit Lions, one of his teammates lost a child to CF, and Steve had put the cause near and dear to his heart. As part of the pre-tournament publicity, he came to Tulsa to shoot a commercial in our backyard with Lo. She was the Sooner Chapter's poster child and a regular attendee of all events.

On the day of the tournament, Lo and I drove to Oklahoma City for the festivities. There, she met several other CF kids who were on hand to help with the event. One of them particularly caught Lo's attention. His name was Eric. He was about twelve years old. Tubes connected a constant source of oxygen to Eric's nose, as cystic fibrosis had destroyed most of his lung function. A portable machine, the size of a briefcase, rolled alongside this young man everywhere he went. Lo talked to Eric periodically throughout the day, not about the tubes and machines but about what grade he was in and if he played golf.

On the way home, Lo sat thoughtfully in the car. I wondered what was occupying her mind. I didn't know that she was trying to peer into her own future. Finally, she broke the silence. "Mommy, am I going to die of CF?" she asked.

Suddenly, I was fighting back tears. I pulled off the highway onto the shoulder and turned to look at the five-year-old who was faced with the very adult concern about her own mortality. I chose my words carefully. "Lo, that's why we're working so hard to raise funds. And that's why we're so excited they found the gene. Before now, no one understood much about CF. The scientists believe it will help them figure out what goes wrong in CF so they can fix it. We have a lot of reason to believe there's hope they'll find a cure for you, little girl." I leaned over and kissed her on the cheek.

Though she looked up at me, she didn't say anything. I decided to let her continue her thoughtful silence. I put the car in gear and pulled back onto the highway, wishing I could have given her a resounding message of comfort. What is 'hope' to a child anyway, I thought? Children don't understand the concept of waiting for something in the distant future. They don't appreciate the abstract at age five. My assumptions proved erroneous a minute later.

"Mom, let's just not worry about me anymore," she declared with her sweet smile and twinkling blue eyes. "Let's raise money so that Eric won't have to carry that big machine around with him everywhere. That wouldn't be fun at all."

Lo's statement reflected maturity far beyond my own. In a sense, she had realized that the future was not as important as the present, and at the present her new friend needed help. "You know, Lo," I smiled back, through tears of pride, "you are a pretty special young lady. Eric is lucky to have you on his side."

Chapter 22

SLEEPLESS NIGHTS

unning parallel to our search for a CF cure was our quest for a good night's sleep. CF was Public Enemy Number One, but by the beginning of the 1990's, insomnia had clearly established itself as Public Enemy Number Two. Insomnia was a disease which struck us just as CF struck Lo. For years, we had been able to minimize its impact on our lives. But insomnia is not just one or two sleepless nights. It is one more sleepless night on top of many others. It has a cumulative affect.

Sleep had been a hit-and-miss affair for me long before cystic fibrosis invaded our lives, so it should have been no surprise that the added burden of Lo's illness disrupted my sleep cycle even more. Unfortunately, insomnia gradually began to claim Terry's midnight hours as well. What should have been a temporary break in her ability to recuperate from our children's infancies turned into an unbroken chain of wakefulness.

Too often, it was like we were zombies, going through the motions of living in a desperate attempt to maintain the appearance that we were coping adequately with our situation. We managed to struggle through the days, bleary-eyed and weary-minded. The evenings were far more of a challenge, as we were running on mere fumes of energy. But as bedtime would draw near, the exhaustion that accompanied us every hour of the day would be replaced by a sudden surge of adrenalin, depriving us of the rest we so desperately needed.

"Hi, Daddy!" Both girls screamed as I rolled into the garage one night after work. Terry, too, stood at the door smiling. I should have responded to their greeting with equal delight. In my heart of hearts, I wanted to leap out of the car and grab each one of them up in my arms. These were my ladies, the most important people in my life. Their eyes shone with anticipation, as if my presence really offered them a reason to be excited.

But the long, trying day I'd had at the office left me with barely enough energy to pull myself out of the driver's seat. The scant hours of sleep I'd had the night before had given me nothing to draw from during the conference calls, meetings with clients and documents I'd had to produce. My knees ached; my head throbbed. I sighed and mustered a quiet, "Hello girls."

Terry understood without an explanation. "Girls, let Daddy get in the door for a few minutes, okay? Just give him time to change clothes. You go play."

It made me sick that I had all but rejected their welcome. But experience had taught me that anger was simmering just below the surface of exhaustion. A few minutes of changing gears in my room usually helped me push back the ragged edginess to a depth where I would be less apt to overreact to some insignificant incident.

Terry followed me to the bedroom, sinking into a chair in the corner. I loosened my tie enough to pull it over my head. I unbuttoned the shirt that had been choking me all day long. I couldn't wait to get it off and ram it into the drawer where we put our dry cleaning. I hung my jacket and pants up and grabbed the jeans hooked behind the door. As I stretched the armholes of one of my dozens of t-shirts, I glanced over at our bed. Suddenly, I felt the overwhelming urge to lie down and sleep. My eyes were heavy, the thought of sleep like a magnet, pulling me towards the bed in which I had so desperately lain awake the night before. I fought against the urge, knowing that I had only a few hours to spend with my family, to rest, relax, re-group. That is, if I could restrain the irritability that wrestled with my more loving intentions. More than anything, I hoped that this intoxicating sleepiness would return at bedtime.

"Long day?" Terry had been watching me silently till now. I didn't answer. She didn't press the issue.

I leaned over and chose some tennis shoes. Not like it was a choice. It was the same pair of tennis shoes I put on every single night. I sat on the corner of the bed to tie the laces, noticing that even this small task seemed to sap the strength from my fingers.

"When is dinner?" I asked, emotionless.

"Doesn't really matter to me," Terry said. "I just have to heat the rolls."

I sighed again, heavily. "Every day is so long when you don't sleep."

"I know what you mean. It's a tired feeling that's just plain scary. You think any minute you could totally lose control —

go crazy — off the deep end."

The girls' giggles from the room down the hall turned to bickering. "Lo, I had that first. Give it back to me."

"You said I could borrow it, Janie. I'm not done with it yet."

"It's mine, Lo. You're going to ruin it if you play with it like that."

I didn't have any idea what the issue was. I just knew I couldn't listen to them argue another second. Sensing my impatience, Terry headed toward the room. "Girls, not now. Jane, go set the table. Lo, pick up the toys and come help me serve dinner. And don't say another word."

Sadly, I followed them out to the kitchen. It was my own weariness that was causing this distress, I thought guiltily. Like wearing the same pair of shoes, every night seemed to follow the same scenario. Tension ruled the tenor of our home. And, to make matters worse, it wasn't only insomnia with which we were dealing. It was the rigorous routine that demanded strict adherence. First there was dinner and making sure Lo took all her medicines. Then there was homework for Jane and the usual bath time ritual that most families with small children have. On top of this were the demands of breathing treatments and physical therapy for Lo, followed by more medications and inhalers. Finally, we'd be ready for bedtime and the attendant prayers, stories and hugs.

Inevitably about the time Terry and I would collapse for a few minutes of television and conversation, Jane would reappear out of her bedroom hoping for a few extra minutes of our time. "Go to bed, Jane. Now!" we'd yell, too often ending the night with resentment.

Then, slowly but surely, the cloud of exhaustion would lift, leaving us in a state of high alert. We'd continue to go through the motions of preparing ourselves for bedtime, turning out lights and climbing under covers, exchanging hugs and saying goodnight. But instead of drifting off to sleep, mysteriously, we were transformed into mind-motoring maniacs, with the depressing realization that another night had begun. Another sleepless night.

"You awake?" I said in a normal speaking voice one night after lying motionless for hours.

"Totally."

"I lie here frozen, absolutely still so I won't disturb you in case you've fallen asleep. I count sheep — I think I'm up to a million. I try to pray. Nobody answers. I meditate — till my mind starts racing. I do everything in the whole world but fall asleep."

"I know. Me, too. I'm so tired all day long I can barely stay awake in the afternoon."

"Try concentrating on fifty pages of microprint."

"Yeah, well, no thanks. I can't stay awake watching the girls, much less wade through reams of legalese."

"So, why can't we sleep, Terry? What are we doing wrong anyway?"

Silent anguish pervaded our thoughts. Finally, Terry offered, "I think for me the answer's simple. My body has forgotten how to stay asleep. It can't trust the possibility anymore. I'm like a lab mouse, except instead of reacting to an electric shock, I'm jolted by the sound of my little girl choking to death, cough by cough. I think my body is traumatized by the constant disruption. I can't ignore the sound. Guilt catapults me out of bed and into her room, as if anything I could do would possibly combat cystic fibrosis."

It was true. Nearly every night Terry would spring out of bed at the first sound of hacking. On those nights when the coughing continued ceaselessly, I, too, would follow her into Lo's room, ready to offer assistance where I could. Preparing breathing treatments, tracking down inhalers and doling out cough medicine left us wide-awake, though totally drained. It happened night after night.

But honestly, I couldn't say that was the main reason for my inability to sleep. More often than not, Terry was the midnight caregiver. She insisted that I stay in bed and rest since I still had to go earn a living every morning.

I suspected that the basis for my insomnia was attributable to a deeper source, but I hadn't yet been able to identify it. I only knew that, melded in with the exhaustion, the anger, and the weariness was a subtle awareness of discontentment and frustration, even bitterness. I was beginning to feel as if the weight of the world was resting squarely on my shoulders. I felt somehow responsible for finding answers to questions I found it hard to even ask. I thought I had to make things right for myself, my family — and for Lo. But I was frankly too tired to know how to begin.

Fortunately, in an almost absurd way, the endless nocturnal hours Terry and I spent in aimless conversation brought us closer than ever. They provided us with an opportunity to talk about everything from sex to current events, the girls and our future. But eventually, the conversation would reach a lull. Terry would finally drift off.

As happened frequently, I would give up on the idea of sleep. I'd slip out of bed, get dressed as quietly as I could, and pull the door of our bedroom shut behind me. I'd tip-toe down the hall, across the family room floor to the kitchen, where I'd throw on a jacket, slip my car keys off the wall rack and head to the garage.

"Hi Don!" the graveyard shift clerk would greet me at the

Homeland grocery store near our house. "Not sleeping again?"

"You got it," I'd wave. A package of chocolate chip cookies and a quart of milk later, I'd finally stumble back to bed, stuffed and disgusted. Now, sleep would finally overtake me. About the time that I'd begin to really relax, the alarm clock would go off, reminding me that it was time to do it all over again.

Chapter 23

TRIUMPHS AND TRIBUTES

*T*wo things have marked the growth of the Sooner Chapter of the Cystic Fibrosis Foundation. One has been the oftentimes-extraordinary response of the entire Tulsa community to a very worthy cause. The other has been the enduring nature of the commitment.

As the years piled one upon the other, our relationships with CF volunteers created bonds that far surpassed typical friendships. Ages and backgrounds were irrelevant as we simply enjoyed the fun and fellowship of working together. And each time any of us looked at Lo or in the faces of other innocent children whose lives were so impacted by the cruelty of cystic fibrosis, we redoubled our efforts on their behalf. For Don and me the choice was obvious. We felt we had a responsibility to Lo to help raise funds for research. But we never took for granted the outpouring of generosity from others who joined our fight because of our child and others like her.

Breakthroughs in medical research heightened our awareness of the need for additional funds to maintain the pace of progress. "The only thing between us and a cure is money," was *a phrase used frequently by the national foundation as a motivator to volunteers. This came on the heels of the announcement that the genetic marker had been found and continues to this day.*

Our chapter historically responded to the call by tapping into our imaginations. Who did we know that could support our cause? What resources did we have that could create interest for potential donors? As the All Sports Ball was still our largest fundraiser, we often used this event to put our findings to work. Since the major part of the income for the event came from the proceeds of a silent and a live auction, we tried to think of items to auction off that buyers would not otherwise be able to acquire.

"Alma, do you think there's any way you could ask Mr. Walton to help us with a fundraiser?" My mom and I and the girls had taken a longtime friend out for lunch. Alma's children, my sisters, Ginny and Susie, and I had spent years together on a local competitive swimming team. Every summer morning and many winter nights we would work out at area pools. Throughout the year, we would spend weekends at swimming meets. Our families grew close and still keep in touch. The Robson family was one of many examples of friends who rushed to our side when Lo was diagnosed and have remained there ever since. It so happened that Alma's husband, Nick, was related to the founder of Wal-Mart, Sam Walton. "We were wondering if maybe he would be willing to let us auction him and his wife off for dinner."

"Sure, I suppose I could ask him," Alma said. "He has a tremendously busy schedule, but what's the worst that could happen? He'd just say no, right? In fact, we're having a family reunion next month. Maybe I can get him aside there."

Shortly after her return, we got a phone call from Alma. "Well, I talked to Sam at the reunion. He's going to do it! He can't believe anyone would want to pay money just to eat dinner with him," she laughed. "But he said since it was a cause that would help children, he'd be happy to participate." She was as surprised and excited as we were.

With the help of a couple whose home would provide a magnificent site for the December holiday dinner, and the culinary expertise of our friends Cheryl Thomas and Dee Dee Hill, we auctioned off a dinner for eight at the All Sports Ball two months later. Four couples gladly paid nearly $4,000 to have dinner with the country's wealthiest and most famous entrepreneur.

The evening was made all the more memorable when the guests of honor had not arrived fifteen minutes after they were scheduled. It was bitterly cold outside and there were icy patches on the streets. Knowing that the Waltons were driving in from Bentonville, Arkansas, and then stopping at Alma and Nick's house, we worried that perhaps they'd had car trouble or had gotten lost. In addition to all the individuals who had spent months arranging the dinner, eight people had contributed a great deal of money to be there. I was a nervous wreck. Finally, the doorbell rang. Jack, the host, opened the door just as a white-haired gentleman peeked in. "Would you be having a dinner here, tonight?" he asked humbly.

Recognizing the well-known figure, Jack extended his hand and replied, "Yes, sir. We are having a dinner here in your honor, Mr. Walton!"

Relieved, the famous businessman nodded, turned around and stepped back out onto the front porch to summon his wife. Cupping his hands together, he yelled, "Helen, this here's the place."

The evening turned out to be a glorious success, thanks to the cooperation of Alma, Mr. and Mrs. Walton, who came all the way from Arkansas, the people who bought the dinner, the couple who hosted the event, Cheryl, who flew down from Michigan,

Dee Dee, and many others. Their efforts in going to extraordinary lengths created an evening that was spectacular and unforgettable for all.

In fact, it was during this year that Don served as president of the Sooner Chapter. He had long observed many meritorious acts of service to our local foundation. He also noticed that individuals were only recognized if they chaired an event. Don decided to rectify the situation. He had particularly noticed one individual, whose presence had been leaving an impact long before Don and I had even heard of cystic fibrosis. Tom Boyd had contributed to the success of the chapter in as many ways as any individual possibly could. Don decided that it was time to recognize him in a special way. Tom was not only a constant in the activities of the chapter, he and his wife, Jean, were also the parents of the oldest surviving patient in our area. Their son, Chris, had fought the ravages of cystic fibrosis for nearly thirty years. The Boyds had been active in CF fundraising ever since Chris's diagnosis. It was primarily because of them that our chapter was founded.

Don wanted to tie Tom's service to CF in with the spirit that seemed to be synonymous with the organization. He knew there was another individual who had contributed mightily to the bottom line of our chapter since its inception. He was Henry Zarrow. It was Henry and his wife, Anne, who had helped create such excitement over the All Sports Ball the year prior to Lo's diagnosis. Don decided that the best way to honor Tom was to create an award called the Henry Zarrow Award and make Tom its first recipient.

He asked Lo and me to go down to Henry's office and ask permission to use his name for such a purpose. I will never forget taking my little girl downtown to the skyscraper where "Mr. Henry" worked.

"Mommy, can I push the button?" Lo asked as we stepped inside the elevator.

"Sure," I answered, lifting her up and directing her finger to the twenty-first floor indicator. As we stepped out into the lobby of the Sooner Pipe and Supply Corporation, I felt a sudden awe. Mr. Henry was one of the most successful businessmen in the city. His name was a household word. I had met him only a couple of times and though he had always been gracious, I was as nervous as if I were getting ready to confer with the president of the United States.

"It's nice to see you, Mrs. Detrich," he greeted me as if I were the celebrity, taking my hand in both of his. "And how are you today, Lo," he came over and patted Lo's hand. "Would you like to sit in my lap? I don't have such pretty ladies calling on me too often."

"Okay," Lo smiled, regarding her new friend with a grin. I watched the instantaneous bonding of the two as I sat down in a chair opposite his desk. Mr. Henry was soft-spoken and gentle as a lamb. I decided he must look like Abraham in the Bible. Lo was as comfortable with him as she would have been with a grandparent.

"Mary," Mr. Henry buzzed his secretary, "would you have something special for these ladies from us?"

"Yes, sir," came the reply. "I'll be right in."

A minute later, she entered the office bearing two packages, wrapped in paper and tied with ribbon. She handed one to Lo and one to me.

"Oh, a present!" Lo giggled excitedly. "Can I open it?"

"I wish you would," Mr. Henry answered. "I want to see it again."

"And me, too?" I joined in the fun.

"Certainly," Mr. Henry replied.

My package contained a lovely bottle of perfume. Lo opened her box to find an adorable stuffed dog. "Thank you, Mr. Henry," she said in delight. She reached up to him with her free arm and hugged him around the neck.

"You have certainly made my day," he smiled.

"You are too kind," I said. "With a reception like this, we could be regular visitors."

Mr. Henry smiled again.

"Mr. Henry, we have a very important purpose for visiting you today," I didn't want to take up too much of his time. "As this year's chapter president, Don has decided we need to recognize a very special volunteer who has perhaps contributed more to our efforts than anybody — Tom Boyd."

"He's the reason I got involved with cystic fibrosis in the first place," Mr. Henry nodded his head.

"Then I'm sure you know all of this already," I said. "Since we became involved, Don has watched Tom. He does it all. He's willing to assume positions of leadership, identify major funding sources, counsel volunteers or staff members, solicit auction items, set up at events and clean up long after everyone else has gone home. He figures out a way to introduce himself or greet every single person at a meeting, fundraiser, or party and then make each person feel special in a very genuine way. He recognizes that they all bring a valuable gift to our organization just by being there."

"He's a true gentleman," Mr. Henry agreed, "one who understands teamwork." Lo just sat on his lap contentedly listening.

I continued. "No doubt Tom has never expected any kind of recognition. But Don thinks it's time to let him know how much his contributions to CF are appreciated. And since you're someone who Tom loves and respects, Don decided that giving him an award bearing your name would serve to honor both of you."

"That is very generous," Mr. Henry said seriously. "We give to cystic fibrosis to help children like Chris Boyd and my friend Lo, here. Right, Lo?" He gave her a squeeze. "Nothing makes my wife and I happier than to help other people. My brother, Jack, feels the same way. Our family has been very blessed to be in the position we're in."

"So is it all right with you that the chapter institutes a Henry Zarrow Award?"

"Yes, ma'am. I would be honored."

As it turned out, Mr. Henry presented the award to Tom during the chapter's annual meeting the next month. Tom was astounded. In years to come the award came to symbolize the highest achievement in our chapter and would also be given to other individuals whose contributions reflected Tom's inexhaustible commitment to funding cystic fibrosis research.

Chapter 24

GREAT FAMILY
VACATION

Lo was six years old before Terry and I considered taking the great American adventure — a family vacation. As the amount of equipment required to administer Lo's needs grew, we had a harder and harder time convincing ourselves that a trip could possibly be worth the effort. But we wanted the girls to see our beautiful country, so we opted to try.

I had a close friend from high school who had settled in Montana. Ray Stinnett and his wife, Michele, had invited us to visit them on numerous occasions. We decided that with careful planning, we could manage the 2,000 miles distance between Tulsa and Bozeman. We laid out the itinerary, then made hotel reservations, giving ourselves plenty of time to reach our destinations, including what we thought was ample leeway for unforeseen circumstances. As the day of departure neared, everything appeared to be in order. We were all excited about the prospects of hitting the road.

Then disaster struck. On the night before we were supposed to leave, Jane walked into our bedroom saying, "I don't feel so good." She was pale as a ghost, and her eyes were extremely bloodshot. Terry took her temperature. It was one hundred and three degrees.

We had planned to get up very early in the morning in order to make it to Denver in time for the girls to swim. Things were heading downhill and we hadn't even left the driveway. We postponed our departure until Terry could get Jane to the doctor.

After a huge injection of penicillin, Dr. Kramer advised us that we could leave. "You can call me from wherever you go. The only concern I have is that this doesn't prompt another more serious infection. If Jane's fever stays high for two or three days, or if she has any facial swelling, take her to a hospital and let them examine her."

With those somewhat-less-than reassuring words, we packed the car. I could hardly believe the amount of space I had to allocate for breathing treatment machines, medications and supplies. Of course, that didn't minimize the baggage my three women found necessary to take. Seven hours later than scheduled, we shoved off.

We saved the entire back seat for Jane to lie down and sleep. Lo was wedged in between us in the front seat amongst maps, purses and water bottles. But at least we were off. I felt a certain sense of accomplishment for a whole four blocks. That was when Lo looked up at me and asked, "Daddy, how long until we get there? I'm kinda bored."

Two hours after leaving, it was time for a breathing treatment. We couldn't anticipate where we were going to be for treatments. We just knew we would need electricity. I spotted an All State insurance office in a small town. "Why not?" I said, pulling into their parking lot. "They are the people with good hands, aren't they?"

Terry stayed in the car with Jane who was feeling worse by the minute. Entering the office, I asked the agent at the desk, "Could we use an outlet to give my little girl a breathing treatment?" I held out the portable compressor.

"Sure," he agreed. Surveying the room, he said, "But I'm afraid our desks are full of papers. I don't know where you'll be able to find room to put your machine."

"No problem," I assured him. "We'll just plug it in and sit on the floor." Thirty minutes later, we were back on the road.

By dinnertime, we had barely reached Wichita. "I think we're going to have to stop here," Terry said glancing at Jane. In order for her to take care of Jane, and allow Lo and me to get some sleep — we rented a two-room suite at a less-than-stellar motel. Throughout the night, I could hear Terry wringing out washcloths as she tried to make Jane more comfortable.

It wasn't until the second night that we made it to Denver. Instead of going for a swim, as we had originally planned, we ended up in the hospital with Jane whose fever had remained extremely high all day. After examining her, the doctor concluded she was merely fighting a wicked virus and gave her a hefty dose of Tylenol. It brought her fever down, though it was only temporary. We moved on.

We had to get gas in Ft. Collins, Colorado. Something must have been going on in town that day because it took half an hour to get through the line. While I waited in the car the girls ran to the restroom. A minute later, they rushed back.

"Daddy, we can't go to the bathroom here!" Jane looked aghast.

"It smells yucky in there," Lo held her nose.

"It is absolutely filthy," Terry shuddered.

We stayed long enough to fuel, with both girls squirming in the back seat. Then we headed to another station. Fortunately, this one's restrooms were satisfactory for my girls. However, another gigantic problem arose.

"Daddy, they don't have the right kind of cups here."

"What could be wrong with them?" I was always baffled by details like this.

"Now, Don, it does make sense to have lids so the drinks don't spill."

I merely shook my head and headed off to a third service station for traveling beverages.

Lo spotted a Dairy Queen a few blocks from the gas station. "Oooh, Daddy, can we get an ice cream cone?"

"No! That's it. We've been in this town for nearly an hour. If we stay any longer, somebody's going to have to go to the bathroom again. We're outta here!" The car was quiet for some time.

The next day, Jane woke up with welcome words. "I think I'm beginning to feel better." It was a good thing because we were wondering if we should just go home. We called the Stinnetts to let them know we had been delayed, but would meet them at Yellowstone, after a short visit with our friends, Bill and Bob Thomas's parents, in Jackson Hole. Although I had to carry Jane most of the way around our walking tour of the national park, things seemed to be turning around. We had persevered and now hoped to enjoy the rest of the trip.

No such luck. Twenty-four hours later, Terry and the girls accompanied Michele to Bozeman while I played golf with Ray at a course in Big Sky. On the way, Lo announced, "Mom, I don't feel so good." Michele took them straight to the doctor in

Bozeman. The opportunistic virus posed even more problems when the "host" had cystic fibrosis. Plus, the doctor had never treated anyone with CF and didn't know much about it.

"Let's put you and Lo on an airplane and Jane and I'll drive the car home," I suggested after a day of letting Lo try to weather the virus on her own. Too often her viruses led to pneumonia. With no CF doctor available, we didn't want to be stranded in Bozeman. An hour later, Jane and I left. The Stinnetts took Terry and Lo to the airport.

The vacation from hell could have ended there but it didn't. Several hours out of Bozeman, I felt myself getting feverish. "Jane, I don't feel so good," I announced dejectedly.

"Daddy, should we stop?"

"No, I think we'd better keep on driving."

Thirteen hours later Jane said, "Daddy, you look awful sleepy. Are you sure you can stay awake all the way home?"

"I'm doing okay," I said, trying to convince myself.

"But you're shaking. I think we need to stop now."

Jane had done a great job of keeping me alert but I knew I had about reached my limit. I shook with a fever so high I could barely drive. "You're right, Jane. We'd better pull off for a while so we can take a little nap."

Several miles down the road, we found a rundown motel with a vacancy. As soon as we checked in to our room, Jane piled the blankets and pillows on me trying to stop my chills. Finally, I drifted off for a few hours. The next day, we drove the rest of the way to Tulsa. I have never been so glad to get home. From vacation.

Two years passed before we were able to look back and laugh. It was at that point that we decided to try another road trip. "Let's go to the beach," Jane suggested. It seemed like a great idea at the time. The girls were older. We were experienced. Little did we know that we were about to embark upon Vacation from Hell, Part Two. This time the car broke down before we even left . . . three hours after departure, we were forced to pull over as it started on fire . . . only to be followed by a half day's delay on I-40 due to a traffic accident . . . and coasting down the Blue Ridge Parkway with the brake warning lights on the whole way . . . you get the idea.

But what family doesn't have vacation stories like these? Actually, the times we shared on vacations provided us with memories to treasure all of our lives. They taught us that where there is a will to travel with a chronically ill child, there is surely a way. Vacations have been opportunities to make an event the focus of our activities rather than the disease of cystic fibrosis. They made us feel like a normal family, rather than one defined by illness. We wouldn't have traded them for the world.

Chapter 25

LIKE FATHER,
LIKE DAUGHTER

*W*hen Lo was about to go off to preschool, I hoped she wouldn't be excluded because of her illness. I prayed children wouldn't ridicule her when she had to be excused from class to take medicine or forget her when she had to be absent for days or weeks at a time. I prayed she would resolve to live life as fully as possible. I didn't realize it at the time, but I should have known that God had already seen to these needs. I had only to look at her dad to be reminded that life's challenges can be seen from a perspective that makes them as matter-of-fact as they are momentous. It was so easy to forget that Don had faced cancer, that he had lived most of his life with only one eye. My husband was blessed with tenacity and discipline. Had I forgotten again the inspiration of his past?

I was determined to get back to my regular routine after eye surgery. The morning after I was released from the hospital, I appeared at the kitchen table in my school uniform. "I miss everybody, Mom. I want to go back to school."

My mom later told me she wondered if she should encourage me to wait, both from a physical and emotional standpoint. She worried that the other children might not accept my disability, that they'd make fun of me. She wondered how I would respond to their curiosity about the bandages I wore and what was under them. But she also knew I had always been pretty confident and enthusiastic, that I hated to sit still very long and that being at school might provide me with the activity I needed. She'd been told that the kids had been praying for me every day. She appreciated the daily trips the priest and nuns had made to the hospital, so she decided she could trust my care to them. She took me to school, hoping God would protect me and that my schoolmates would welcome me back.

I returned home elated. "Guess what, mom? They elected me class president while I was gone. Isn't that great?" Much to my parents' relief, it never occurred to me that my classmates might treat me differently just because I had lost my eye.

Soon I began to tackle my biggest post-surgery challenge. I didn't know it but Mom watched through the kitchen window as I sauntered out the back door to the basketball hoop, which was mounted above the garage. My head was still covered with bandages, but I couldn't wait any longer to try and make a basket.

Mom could see from my shots that I had no idea where the ball was in relation to the basket. Playing sports was my favorite thing in the world, but as Dr. Newell had said, I no longer had any depth perception. She wondered how I could possibly compete with other kids who had no disabilities. This devastating thought was compounded when I turned around. The bandages taped around my head were filled with blood. Horrified, Mom rushed outside. "Donny, are you okay?"

"Sure, Mom. I just can't seem to figure out how to get the ball through the hoop," I grinned, oblivious to the scene my eye was creating. I couldn't understand why she was so upset. I knew I wasn't in any pain, and I was happy to finally handle a ball again. "I've got to keep playing, Mom. I'm tired of doing nothing."

A call to Doctor Newell reassured my mother that the overexertion would postpone healing, but wouldn't cause any permanent damage. He encouraged her to restrict my level of activity to a minimum. I remember seeing my mom hang up the phone, then just stand there looking at it. I know now that she was weighing the difference between the doctor's orders and her little boy's dreams. Instinct told her that my determination to regain my skill should temper the protective restrictions recommended by Dr. Newell. Finally she sighed and turned to me. It must have been hard for her, but she simply said, "Practice makes perfect, honey!"

As the weeks turned into months, visits back to the eye clinic downtown grew less frequent, but the threat of cancer didn't really begin to diminish until after the six-month examination. Mom and Dad told me later that this is when they first dared to believe I still had a future, though my eye would have to be watched until I was nineteen. They allowed themselves to focus on my ability to handle life with one eye instead of fearing the cancer's return.

I continued to practice re-learning skills. I tried to explain what it was like to my dad. "It feels like I'm a lot heavier on one side. Like I'm off balance or something." Day after day, week after week, I stood in the driveway shooting baskets or playing baseball. Little by little, I learned to adjust to my lack of depth perception. And slowly, but more and more frequently, the ball went in the bucket, or made contact with the bat. Eventually, I was able to regain my skills, and even to develop them far beyond where they'd been before.

When the tissue healed around where my eye had been removed, it was time to be fitted for a prosthesis. Again, we were fortunate. An excellent group of ocularists was located right in downtown Chicago. The process of making the new "eye" took several days. I got to ride the train downtown by myself and meet Dad at the ocularist's office. There we met with the staff who had the task of creating a new likeness of my old eye. We watched, fascinated, as the artists made impressions, carefully measuring and filing the mold into the perfect shape. Then, mixing black and yellow, red and blue, they patiently painted layer after layer of color onto the plastic surface. When they were finished, I peered at myself in the mirror. "Well, I guess it looks like it should, but it feels like a rock's in my head. What do you think, Dad?"

He scrutinized me carefully. He knew I couldn't see out of the prosthesis, but to the rest of the world, I must have looked reasonably normal. It was as good a replacement as he could have gotten for me anywhere. "I think you look like a tiger!" he beamed.

Compared to other children, however, I guess my life wasn't quite as normal as it seemed. We spent most of our summer afternoons at the neighborhood swimming pool. Swimming races, pool games and diving were our favorite activities. The first time I wore my prosthesis to the pool, I dove into the inviting blue water with both eyes open, as I'd always done. Immediately, I felt the suction pull my prosthesis out. As I surfaced, I located the nearest lifeguard. "I've lost my eye!" I yelled.

"You lost WHAT?" responded the guard.

Mom, close by, overheard the remark. "Oh, no!" She rushed over and explained the situation. By this time, the entire group of teenaged workers had gathered around.

"What does it look like?" one of them asked Mom, a little sheepishly. She explained that it was white plastic, and that the iris was painted blue on one side to look like an eye.

"Clear the pool!" announced one of the lifeguards.

Soon all of them had submerged into the water, searching for the missing eye. Finally, it was discovered upside-down on the bottom of the deep end. One of the guards had felt it by sheer luck, as its translucent surface blended in perfectly with the water. I never dove in the pool with my eyes open again.

I often tried to make light of my situation. I discovered that if I adjusted my prosthesis, I could appear to be looking in opposite directions at the same time. I could also take a pencil and tap on it. Those who weren't aware that my eye was plastic were absolutely amazed! I would even have been happy to take it out for "show and tell" sessions at school had the nuns allowed it.

I never thought that losing an eye was an excuse not to compete. But I did realize I had to work harder than other kids. I didn't want to just play sports — I wanted to excel at them. In high school, I played basketball and ran track, but the one talent I really had was a God-given ability to throw the football.

Prior to my junior year at one of Chicago's largest high schools, I joined several of my friends in the pre-season football tryouts. Throughout the summer practices, my coach, Bob

Lombardi, must have seen something in me that had gone unnoticed by my former coaches.

Each day, he compared my skills with those of another player competing for the first string quarterback position. We knew we were both improving. We both worked hard and were eager to play. I suppose it was the fact that I never hesitated to call the plays when Lombardi gave me the responsibility that caused him to start me.

During the first game of the season, even though I threw two interceptions to initiate my high school career, he didn't lose confidence. He kept me in. In the fourth quarter, I threw four touchdown passes, which set an all-time record for the school.

We went on to two outstanding seasons my junior and senior years. With the help of my team, I was able to set several passing records that remained in the books for over two decades. I was even voted an All-Chicagoland quarterback and was the feature of several articles in local newspapers — the quarterback with one eye. I was recruited by schools throughout the country, but chose to attend the University of Tulsa because of its reputation for throwing the football.

In the summer of 1969, I left Chicago. I had been raised with the loving support of a strong family. I had survived a life-threatening disease. Some people might have considered me as having a disability but I never did see myself that way. I was convinced I had the greatest life a kid could hope to have.

As I reviewed the events of Don's past, I had to smile at the thought that there were people who had known him for years who didn't realize he had only one eye. Sometimes, even I forgot. Except when I was mad at him. Then I could make faces at him

on his left side and he didn't even know it.

Yes, Lo had inherited the gene for cystic fibrosis from both of her parents but I hoped she'd also inherited her dad's attitude. I hoped she, too, would see herself as a victor, not a victim. That, I was sure, would enable others to see her as the extraordinary child we knew as our little "Lo."

Chapter 26

MEANING OF
NORMAL

*W*e regularly recalled Dr. Kramer's warnings that chronic disease impacted both the patient and family. At the same time we adamantly wanted to be "normal." Yet, years of living with CF had proved the truth of Dr. Kramer's comments. The tension level in our house was always high, reflected in scene after scene of daily events. One particular exchange stands out.

"Jane, I spent half an hour folding these clothes so all you had to do was put them away. Now look at them. You had to have literally thrown them in the drawer."

"I like them that way."

I rolled my eyes. "Don't you understand why that would irritate me? I don't have an extra second. I took the time to take care of what was yours and now that time's been wasted. Besides, these clothes aren't free, young lady. If you treat them this way, they won't last as long."

"Mom, what difference does it make how long they last? I'm growing out of them every year anyway."

"Because someone else may wear them after you, Jane."

"No matter what I do, it isn't good enough for you."

"That's not true."

"Then why are you always mad at me?"

"Jane, you're missing the point. Can't you understand how we need to pull together as a team? Can't you see that I don't have time to do things just so you can undo them?"

"Then don't," Jane reasoned simply.

If CF hadn't been part of the picture, Jane's comment would probably have made me laugh. As it was, I interpreted her words as oppositional and disrespectful, demanding my authoritarian stance.

"That's it. From now on you'll do your own laundry. You're nine years old. I think you can handle it."

"Oh boy!" Jane responded as if this directive was a dream come true.

"Have I lost my mind? Am I expecting too much from her?" I asked Don later that night.

"We're probably both expecting too much from her," Don said. "It's the situation. But lately I have felt like you could cut the air in here with a knife. Something's got to give. Maybe it's you and me. Let's just see how it works out."

It didn't take long to observe that Jane's laundering habits were going to be unorthodox at best. She would wait until she had nothing to wear, then cram as much as she could into the washer at once, regardless of color. She would take her laundry directly out of the dryer, stuff it into any drawer available, and then rummage through the mass of wrinkles, never considering ironing a thing. Though her clothes all eventually took on a decidedly gray tone and she oftentimes wore outfits that had permanent creases, I was secretly proud of the fact she had risen to the challenge.

Still, I felt guilty. "Maybe I'm too lazy," I confessed to Don. "Maybe I should spend more time helping Jane. But I have to admit, it's easier having her do it than arguing with her about how it should be done."

"Terry," Don said. "It's not worth it. You're already exhausted. Besides, you're never going to teach Jane how to do laundry. She's convinced she already knows. Remember, she's the one that says wrinkled clothes are more comfortable."

"Oh, Don. She just says that to irritate me."

"Listen," my practical husband shook his head. "You told her to do her own laundry because she messed up everything you did for her. I thought your idea was a pretty good one. Stick with it."

"But you don't think I should set an example for her?"

"I think this is one of those things that doesn't matter enough to fight about. Save your energy for the real mountains. We have enough of those to climb."

On other days, our own frustrations sent us over the edge.

"Daddy, be careful around Mommy. I don't think she's in a very good mood," I overheard whispers from Lo one afternoon when I'd slammed the garage door hard enough to break the handle. I don't remember what event caused me to snap. I do recall the humiliation I felt at breaking the handle. As a reminder of that momentary lapse of sanity, we never replaced it.

"Mommy, what's the matter with Daddy?" Jane asked another night, as Don wearily slumped in a dark corner of the living room, unresponsive to anyone. Again, the particular incident that caused his retreat has long been forgotten. But there was no question as to the underlying fomenter of distress. It was as if we were all held prisoner by this captor called cystic fibrosis.

For Lo, the captor was far more tangible. People knew she had the disease. They could see her taking medicines, hear her cough, visit her during hospitalizations. They asked about her state of health constantly.

It wasn't as apparent to others that Lo's illness impacted us as well. But it did. It drained us, tested our wit, and challenged everything we knew about life. The maelstrom created by the constant demands of chronic illness prevented our participation in many social and civic activities. Usually we were simply too tired to go out or entertain guests in our home. It was like we'd been exiled at a time of life when we should have been building relationships, making lifetime memories with other families. "I just don't have enough energy," I'd complain to Don when he would suggest inviting some couples over for dinner.

"Terry, you don't have to spend three months preparing a feast. They don't care what you serve. Have everybody bring something."

"No," I said. "I'm too tired to think about it. Let's just go out."

We never lost the desire to be normal. But we did realize over the years that circumstances dictated we redefine "normal" to suit our situation. The expectation that our family be like other families was unrealistic. We had to accept that "normal" simply means we experienced love and laughter, as well as anger and heartache. At least we hoped our children would remember there were times when laughter shook the household, when we played card games, or had tickling sessions, or watched movies together, cuddled up in the family room.

And though we didn't always exhibit model-parenting skills, we knew we were trying incredibly hard. We were very free with hugs. Our children heard we loved them on a daily basis. They saw us hug one another. And, we were there, day in and day out — for them, for each other. Every night for dinner, at bedtime for prayers, during stormy nights when lightning flashed and thunder shook the house. Irritable, too often. Tired, regularly. But present, always.

Time would reveal whether we were normal enough to remain intact as a family. But every now and then, signs provided promising glimpses that cystic fibrosis would not succeed in destroying the family unit we were desperately trying to maintain. For Don and me there was the knowledge that our marriage was succeeding, that our relationship continued to grow in spite of the challenges we were facing. From Jane there was a wellspring of compassion signaling an awareness of the need to help others. Never willing to divulge her innermost thoughts about Lo's condition, Jane instead demonstrated abundant patience towards her little sister as well as all children younger than herself.

"Will you teach me to skate, Janie?" Lo asked one summer day.

"Yeah, I can do that," Jane agreed. For the next several days, she faithfully strapped Lo's feet into her new birthday roller skates, a feat which was impressive in and of itself, since Jane was only nine at the time. Holding tightly onto each of Lo's wrists, Jane pulled her around and around the garage. All the while, she taught her, "Slide one foot. Now slide the other. Keep pushing down while you slide."

"This is fun, Janie!"

In between, I would hear, "Ouch, Lo!" as a little foot would lose control, sending a rock-hard skate into one or the other of Jane's shins.

"I'm sorry," Lo would apologize sincerely.

Without even letting go to assess the damage, Jane would respond, "It's okay. Just push your foot down." I was impressed that Jane understood innately what to say. It made perfect sense.

And her endurance was heroic. I would have given up after one bruise. Jane was undaunted and it wasn't long before Lo learned to skate.

Soon, Jane set up obstacle paths for Lo to tackle. In time, she taught Lo to skate backwards and even do spins. The first time Lo was invited to a skating birthday party, she looked like a future roller derby queen. Taking time out only now and then to swill down a glass of lemonade, she raced round and round the rink, forwards and backwards. When the announcer drew the party together for games, Lo won blue ribbons for all the speed races.

"Where did you learn to skate like that?" parents and friends alike asked her.

She smiled proudly and said, "My sister taught me." Perhaps they didn't appreciate the truth behind Lo's simple answer but I did. I knew the hours of patient instruction, the bruises, the hero who would, but for a little sister's comment, go forever unsung. "Way to go, Jane," my heart sang. I couldn't have wanted to be part of a family more normal than this.

Chapter 27

LITTLE MISSIONARY

*S*ummer-kissed tendrils of baby fine hair fell softly around Lo's gentle face, her attention focused intently on a sheet of paper lying in her lap. Cheeks, almost alabaster, betrayed her otherwise contented expression. A catheter threaded through her veins was hidden beneath brightly colored dressings. Plastic tubing connected her forearm to a gleaming tree of chrome standing next to the hospital bed. Bags, filled with clear liquid, hung from the chrome branches. Once again, drop-by-drop, the liquid soldiers were battling the infection within her lungs.

Undaunted by her tethers, unconcerned at the mechanism casting a shadow over her diminutive figure, her small fingers clutched tightly around a blue marker, steering it one direction, then another, leaving squiggles, circles and triangles sitting precisely on the page's lines. "Mommy, look! I can write," Lo glanced up at me with delight.

"You certainly can," I admired her work. "I've never seen such tiny intricate writing, either. It's very pretty."

"Thank you," my radiant blue-eyed beauty grinned, switching her blue marker for a green one. "I have to practice for school. Do you think they'll remember me when I go back to kindergarten?"

"I don't think anyone could forget you, honey."

In the beginning, Lo's eyes hinted at the charismatic charm that lay within. She looked directly at everyone, sometimes it seemed right through to a person's heart. It was never in a judgmental way; rather it was as if she was trying to relate to who they were, her genuine interest being paramount.

As her personality began to develop we discovered the extraordinary depth with which she was endowed. She had a tendency to reach out to others, unlike most young children whose worlds naturally revolve around themselves. She asked questions, listened attentively to answers. Her attitude always made people feel special, as though she was glad their paths had crossed hers. Consequently, they, too, were intrigued and eager to respond to her attention, as if her perspective might provide them with personal insight.

At the same time, it was obvious that Lo was equally in touch with something that resonated deep within her own being. She was born with a gift of faith that far surpassed the teaching she was receiving from us. We dutifully instituted mealtime grace and bedtime prayers, and attended church beginning in our children's infancies, but we knew Lo's communication with God extended beyond family rituals and church. Don and I were still molding our own understanding of faith. We were groping with questions of why beauty and truth existed side by side with pain and suffering. For Lo, faith was synonymous with Truth, while pain and suffering were simply a part of life — like eating and sleeping.

With all of the prodding and poking to which she was subjected, we would have thoroughly understood if Lo had been terrified of doctors, lab visits and hospitalizations. She was not. As we watched, as others watched, we learned that Lo's trust in God's care carried her through trials and offered lessons in faith, the kind of childlike faith that stupefies reason. I became aware of how inspiring her faith could be to others during Lo's hospitalization in November of her kindergarten year.

Dr. Kramer had put Lo on an intravenous medication called Tobramycin. The dosage far exceeded that which would be recommended for an otherwise healthy individual. Research had been indicating that mega doses were more effective at treating CF patients' cases of pneumonia. However, the appropriate amount for each individual had to be monitored in order to maintain the optimum amount of drug in the patient's body at all times. This necessitated that blood levels be drawn several times a day.

The infusion schedule for intravenous therapy fell at twelve-hour intervals, in between doses of a different kind of antibiotic. One particular day, Don had spent the night with her and left for the office early in the morning. I couldn't get to the hospital until I had dropped Jane off at school. Meanwhile, a lab tech had come into Lo's room to draw the initial blood sample. It was the first time we had not been there to hold her hand for such a procedure.

As I rounded the corner into the room, Lo flashed a huge grin. "Mom, God helped me not be scared!" she said excitedly. "The lady took my blood and you weren't even here, but God was." My guilt at not being there for her melted as I looked into her shining eyes. It was obvious that she had experienced a strength far greater than I could offer and I remembered the promise — "Lo, I am with you always."

"What did you do, honey?" I wrapped my arms around her tightly.

"I'll show you in a little while," she promised. "The nurse is coming back after the IV is done to get some more blood." Two hours later, the infusion was finished. The phlebotomist returned with her cart full of vials and needles.

"How's our little angel now?" she smiled warmly at Lo as she prepared her supplies.

"I'm great," Lo said. "My mommy's going to watch you this time."

The woman looked at me. "I suppose you know you have a very special child," she said seriously. "I've never seen anything like it."

"We think we'll keep her," I answered, curious to see what Lo would do next.

"I just hate sticking kids," the tech said as she flushed Lo's catheter with saline solution and heparin. After attaching a new needle to an empty vial, and opening a fresh alcohol pad, she looked at Lo. "Now are you ready to get this over with again?" I could see the cloud of regret in her eyes as she looked for the vein from which she hoped to draw blood.

"Can you wait a minute?" Lo asked politely.

"I can." The woman smiled at me.

Lo closed her eyes and folded her hands. We watched her mouth a silent prayer. "Okay, I'm ready," she held out her arm to the tech confidently.

Nervously, the woman rubbed Lo's forearm, then swabbed it. I could see her own hands were shaking. I knew she hoped to repeat the success she had apparently had earlier. She inserted the tiny needle into Lo's forearm, while Lo watched intently.

Seeing Lo's apparent interest in the proceeding, the tech said, "I can't believe you watch. I think I'm more nervous than you are." She drew back the syringe and breathed a sigh of relief as blood began to fill the vial.

All the while, Lo's eyes were calmly fixed on the needle in her arm. As the tech withdrew the needle and applied a band-aid to the site, Lo congratulated her. "You did a good job. Thank you."

The woman laughed. "Why thank you, little lady!" Glancing at me, she added, "She's just amazing. She's so young. Most kids scream and holler the whole time. She's a better patient than most grown-ups. And, come to think of it, I've never had a child thank me for doing this before."

The next time she came back, she brought a small entourage of phlebotomists. They all watched Lo say her little prayer, then look directly into the eyes of the tech while confidently holding out her arm. They smiled as she again thanked her for doing a good job. "God makes me not scared," she explained when they marveled at her bravery.

Her simple little statement and demonstration of faith said more than the most eloquent sermon. Time and again Lo has shown through such simple words and actions that God's love is as real as pain or fear, and far more powerful.

Chapter 28

IMAGINARY
WORLDS

"*M*ommy, would you like to make an appointment at my office?*" seven-year-old Doctor Lo called from the makeshift desk in her bedroom.*

I pulled another stack of books out from the dark recesses of a cabinet I was cleaning. I had started the afternoon determined to accomplish at least one seasonal task. But Lo's invitation reminded me of a poem a friend had given me when the girls were little. It was about how there will always be time to clean the dust that settles in a house but there is only a short while to enjoy your children, as they grow up and settle elsewhere. It offered a convenient excuse, I had to admit, but it was also wise advice. Plus, I had been hearing Lo's imaginary conversations with nurses and patients. Shoving the books back into the cabinet, I answered, "I've been thinking I should have an appointment, Doctor." I pulled myself up to a standing position, brushed the dust off my hands onto my jeans, and "limped" into Lo's room. "When is the next available opening?"

"Well, we're pretty booked up this afternoon, but you can come at 4 o'clock," the diminutive physician looked over the little mask that was held to her face via an elastic string. The compact air compressor hummed at her side as it forced the medicine in her nebulizer through the tubing into her lungs for the afternoon's breathing treatment. The mist that escaped out the sides of the mask seemed to linger, as if to remind us that there was no way to eliminate the constant intrusion of cystic fibrosis into our lives.

"Four o'clock would be fine," I agreed.

"I think it might save us a little time if we went ahead and opened your file," she suggested. "Can you stay a minute?" She looked up at me with a friendly grin that no mask could hide. Little did she know I would have agreed to stay all day.

"I would appreciate anything that would expedite a doctor's appointment," I smiled. "What do you need to know?" Pulling out a set of file folders and index cards, my doctor went about her job professionally and efficiently. I marveled at the detail to which she had gone into for this make-believe doctor's office.

"Name, please."

"Mary Smith." She took a purple marker and carefully wrote the name down on the appropriate dotted line.

"Address."

I decided I lived in Texas. There was a place for the street address, city, state and zip code.

"Telephone."

I included the area code.

"Do you know your social security number?"

I laughed and gave it to her. I suppressed another laugh as I noticed the "soshl seqraty" spelling she used.

"Now, could you explain your symptoms to me?" She looked dead serious. I glanced down at her chart. The lines and graphs were all there, forms similar to the ones she had seen in Dr. Kramer's office, only a bit more color-coordinated.

"Wow, Doctor, I am impressed," I said and quickly dreamed up a long list of symptoms.

"That's all I need for now," she smiled after I listed my complaints. "We'll see you at four." Pulling the mask off for a second, she whispered, "That's now, Mommy. Could you go out and come back in?"

A few minutes later, I was being examined with toy thermometers, stethoscopes, tongue depressors and the keen senses of my young doctor. The treatment for my limp and an infection she discovered included pills dispensed from an empty enzyme container and a shot given via an old — needle-less — syringe we'd saved from her latest round of home IV therapy. Carefully she wrote down in her own version of medical-ese what she prescribed so that she would have an accurate record for future reference.

"I feel better already," I smiled as I waved good-by.

Some weeks it was being a doctor that captivated Lo's imagination, other weeks it was teaching school, running "The Pricilla Hotel," or solving a case that had baffled the greatest lawyers and detectives in the world. For the school she lined up rows of stuffed animals, each having its own set of materials and name, each occupying a square of the rug in Lo's room which had been designed to look like a quilt. She kept a seating chart and attendance records, which she filed in a drawer. For the hotel, she had a carefully drawn layout of rooms and tablets describing in detail what amenities and features each room contained and a price list for each. As Lawyer Lo, she drew up contracts, which she ran by her dad, to verify that they would be legal documents.

Lo's world was one which was fun to visit — imaginary or real. It was an incredible relief that she was able to entertain herself so creatively during the endless hours she was tied up — both figuratively and literally — with medical treatments. Rather than complain about her limitations, she figured out ways to make the most of the little freedom she had. Generally speaking, she had to spend at least two to three hours every day hooked up to machines. In those days, the crudeness of the compressors and density of the medications prolonged the time it took to inhale the aerosolized liquid. If Lo was also taking IV medications, the hours increased dramatically.

It would have been understandable if she had asked to skip a treatment, or if she had tried to curtail the nebulization, leaving unaerosolized medicine in the container. But instead she accepted whatever demands were made of her, throwing herself totally into her imaginary worlds, her enthusiasm drawing us into her games of pretend with delight. Consequently, we promptly filled her requests for supplies to create her imaginary worlds.

As she grew, the games became more sophisticated, as did the supplies. By the time she was eight, she owned a genuine cash register, given to her by some restaurateur friends. Her inventory included calculators, a menagerie of writing utensils that would rival the office supplies of a discount store, various and sundry kinds of paper, desks and so on.

Her activities weren't always limited to office-type settings, though. One of the most enjoyable activities in which the whole family had the opportunity to participate was when Lo decided to build an airplane and invited us to fly cross-country. Lo served as both the flight attendant and pilot. Though we rode 'first class,' we could see the pilot's cabin from our seats. Every conceivable device in her room served a purpose. An old computer keyboard from Don's office became an instrument panel, an old infant car *toy provided a steering wheel, a bright yellow radio-audiocassette player provided both in-cabin music and communication with the air traffic controller, to whom she spoke using a set of headphones. When the plane was on autopilot she would attend to the passengers seated in the cabin in two rows of child-sized chairs. We were offered snacks, drinks and magazines. Throughout the flight, Lo would explain what was happening both in and out of the airplane. Between her flair for creativity and her sense of humor, we had such a terrific trip that we were all sorry to have to land.*

We were thankful that in spite of the presence of the medical equipment too often at her side, the sound of the compressor humming in the background, and the odious breathing-treatment mist that lingered in the air, nothing was able to hamper Lo's enthusiasm for creating these remarkable imaginary worlds.

Chapter 29

HITTING
BOTTOM

*T*he dew had glistened in the early morning sunlight like freshly fallen snow. The picture that was drawn on this pristine canvas revealed much of how my life had changed by the year 1991.

"I'm about done with golf," I reported to Terry, having just returned from my regular Saturday game. I laid my handkerchief and wallet on the chest of drawers. I retrieved the tees and ball markers from my front pocket, looked at them hard for a minute and set them almost ceremoniously on the handkerchief, reflecting on the dewy images of my morning.

We had been the first group on the course. I walked onto number one green and looked back up the fairway. There were three sets of footprints, side by side by side. Over in the rough by themselves were the parallel lines from the tires of my golf cart.

Terry knew I played with a macho group, guys that carried their bags and played on foot. How far you hit the ball was more important than how straight it went. "I guess insomnia has sucked all the macho out of me. While my buddies hoofed it down the fairway, I was relegated to a golf cart in the rough. While I listened to their laughter and camaraderie, I looked at the empty seat next to me."

I picked up the ball marker again and tapped it on the surface of the bureau. "I tee it up every week with a great attitude. But by the fifth or sixth hole, I feel like the club is swinging me. On the back nine, all I want to do is finish so I can get home and lay down. It's just no fun anymore. My head aches, my knees are sore, and my eye burns so constantly I feel lopsided. Nothing's working." I pulled my socks off and threw them in a pile on the floor. "How can I be so tired every hour of the day and so wide-awake all night long? I never sleep. It's become my mantra. I can't sleep — why can't I sleep — go to sleep. I say it over and over again until I'm sick of hearing it myself. Why? Why won't my body let go?" I sat down wearily on the side of the bed. With great effort, I lifted my legs up onto the mattress, my head sank into the pillow.

The windows were open, allowing the gentle breeze to waft in. The sun was shining outside. I could feel its warmth on my face. The intoxication of sleepiness was suddenly overwhelming. Of course, I remembered bitterly. It's a perfect day. It's the weekend. It's the time when I should be enjoying my family, working in the yard, savoring the moment. Now is the time I get sleepy. Now is when I don't have enough energy to do anything but lie here in this bed.

I had listened to Don's every word. I'd heard them all before, but each time I hoped I would glean some new insight that would help us solve the puzzle. The problem of wakefulness had gradually become a couple problem. I identified clearly with the concept of preferring to be alone. It was easier to control my world if I was the only one in it. But I desperately missed the social commitments, the time for personal growth, and the ability to do something for somebody besides me. I wasn't able to give enough to myself to think about offering help to Don. My world, too, had become lonely and isolated. In addition to that, I felt guilty that Don had to hit the ground running every morning. At least I had the solace of privacy within our home. But I knew that wasn't the choice I would have made had I been facing the world well-rested.

"I don't even know who I am when I look in the mirror anymore," I said, sitting down on the chair next to Don. "The shadows and creases tell the story of a woman I thought I'd never be. I look so severe and stern — and old. What is happening to us?"

"Time is going by. Life is going by. It isn't just the golf club that's swinging me. It's my whole life. I've lost control."

"Add to the list the fact that we never do anything anymore."

"But you won't ever call anybody," Don said.

"You could do that, you know," I retorted.

"I don't get why you have to have two weeks advance notice to throw some hamburgers on."

"I know that," I snapped. "But I think it's nice to have something to look forward to."

"Okay, then, let's have a party."

"When?"

"I don't know. What do you think?"

"I'm too tired to think."

"Big surprise."

"Wait a minute," I stopped. "Listen to us. What are we doing? Arguing over some stupid party we'll never have."

"There's nobody to blame, Terry. It'd be easier if there were."
Don sighed. "Listen. When I die, have them put 'He just got too
tired' on my tombstone."
I had to laugh. The epitaph had more than a ring of truth.

In the past, we had pursued answers to our fatigue problem. We had gone to our doctor and described the situation. "You need something to break the cycle," he'd suggested. "I think you should take sleeping pills for a short time."

Funny thing about sleeping pills — they help for a while. At least you don't lay there hour after hour wide awake. But the drug doesn't allow you to experience the kind of deep, restorative sleep that you need either. You wake up with a kind of hangover, in a headachy, groggy state that is anything but rested and after six months of using the pills on and off, they stopped working for us altogether.

What's more, Terry and I began having sharp pains in our backs. The only thing that relieved the discomfort was tremendous pressure to the exact spot where the pain originated. "We'll try cortisone injections," the doctor suggested this time. "You both have trigger points caused by fibromyalgae. The injections will provide you temporary relief." And so he shot needles filled with medication directly into the tight knots of twisted muscles. The medication mercifully provided respite from the pain. But the shots began to work for shorter periods of time. The doctor was perplexed.

"I can't give you the injections frequently enough. The sleeping pills aren't helping. There is one more thing I can offer. Antidepressants." Terry had already been on antidepressants for muscle spasms. She was convinced they made her gain weight and refused to take them again. I took the pills for a while. I knew I was probably depressed, though the idea that someone thought I was depressed brought me down all the more. The pills made me crazy. I threw them out.

"I don't know what else I can do for you," the doctor said sympathetically. "You're experiencing more distress than your bodies can handle. I'd like you to go see a friend of mine. He's a psychologist."

"But we aren't fighting," I said. "We don't have marital problems. We just can't sleep."

"You might be surprised to find out what's preventing you from sleeping. Sometimes, our bodies respond to situations of stress in strange ways. Psychologists are trained to sort out how you can cope better with your particular circumstances."

We went to the psychologist together. He asked one question. It took us two full sessions to answer. The question was, "I want each of you to help me make a list of all the distressful situations you have faced in your marriage." Over the course of the next two sessions, we talked about Lo's birth, diagnosis, hospitalizations and care. We talked about raising children, the economic crisis which had cost us hundreds of thousands of dollars, the threat of running out of insurance, the burglar, the broken finger, the car theft, our parents' surgeries. We recounted only facts, things that had happened over the course of the last decade or so.

"It's no wonder you're exhausted," the doctor consoled us after listening to our two-hour rendition of events. "What you've been through would exhaust anyone." He put his tablet and pencil down and pushed his chair away from the desk. He stood up and walked toward us, on the way lifting another chair up to bring it nearer where we were sitting.

"You see, we all have only a certain amount of energy — call it fuel — from which to handle our daily lives. When a crisis arises, we use more energy than we would for normal situations. We have four sources of energy — physical, mental, emotional and spiritual. Usually, our lives are balanced enough to use some fuel and then refill the tank. It's only when crises build up that one tank is emptied before it has a chance to fill back up. Then we begin drawing from another tank, even if it's one that wouldn't be preferred for a particular problem. For example, if you've had too many emotionally draining experiences, your body may start relying on your physical energy. In your case, you've been losing sleep, no doubt because all the mental and emotional sources of your energy are tapped out. You've just had too many crises." The doctor didn't have a ready solution to our woes, but his explanation alone lifted my spirits. Our exhaustion was justified. I accepted for the first time that I had earned the right to be tired, sick and depressed.

Until Don and I sat down and listed the calamities that had happened to us over ten years, I hadn't realized how many there had been. I hadn't had time to face one before another would hit. Remembering each disaster, describing its circumstances and consequences, forced me to take time to be sad, to grieve, and to acknowledge the pain that I hadn't allowed myself to feel. In a way, reviewing each event carried with it a kind of funereal reality — and finality, one that offered me the ability to move on with my life.

In the middle of our tenure with the psychologist, another trauma hit our family and at the time, it seemed the crowning blow, the one catastrophe that I thought would destroy me completely.

Terry had been training for the River Run, a CF benefit, for months. When the day came, she set out hoping to finish the six miles in less than an hour. Very quickly she realized there was something drastically wrong. She straggled to the finish line encouraged by the shouts of friends and family, but told me immediately afterwards that she needed to get to a doctor first thing the next week.

The examination by her gynecologist was all too reminiscent of the day we got Lo's diagnosis. He asked her to call me for a consultation that afternoon. He had found a large tumor in her uterus, and recommended that she have a hysterectomy immediately.

"There was no evidence of anything abnormal at your annual exam six months ago," he explained to us. "This is growing too rapidly for comfort. I don't think it's cancerous but only biopsies will provide confirmation. I don't mean to instill a sense of panic by any means but you might want to take the rest of this week to make sure your personal affairs are in order. I can schedule you for surgery as early as next Monday."

Though friends and family came to sit with me in the waiting room, I have never felt so alone in my life. Terry and I had faced the traumas over the years and they had worn both of us down, but at least we had faced them all together. Now, Terry's life hung in the balance and I wondered how I could possibly make it without her — she was my lover, the mother of my children and my best friend.

After four hours of surgery, during which time the doctor removed a seven-pound tumor from Terry's body, he was able to tell us that all was well. Biopsies confirmed the tumor was benign. One more time we had weathered the storm together, and life, exhausting as it was, went on.

Chapter 30

SPECIAL
DELIVERY

*I*n an instant of weakness, Don and I agreed to get the girls a dog. For years, we were able to fend off our children's pleas by saying things like, "Girls, there's just too much to do in this house to have a dog. We can't take any more." Perhaps it was the tone in our voices that convinced them this issue was not up for debate. But as it turned out, the dog we fought so hard against bringing into our home proved to be more a messenger of calm than the source of bedlam.

We'd lost another dog earlier in our marriage. Clyde was a little mixed breed runaway. He was also the first pet I'd ever had. He'd been my constant shadow. When I'd gone into midnight labor with Jane, he'd paced the hallway with me for hours before I woke Don. But Clyde was also a rogue. The minute he'd spy an open door, love and loyalty were left in the dust of little paw prints. Unfortunately, a gate left ajar one afternoon while we were gone proved far too great a temptation for our wanderer. We posted signs and made countless trips to the pound, but never saw Clyde again.

Losing him had been a heartbreaking experience for me. I resolved never to become so attached to another animal. After Lo's birth I convinced myself a similar tragedy would overwhelm my children. As time healed my heartache, the idea of training a puppy and raising two babies sounded like more trouble than it was worth anyway. With cystic fibrosis's intrusion, we were more convinced of this truth than ever. We envisioned the shedding of dog hair throughout the house, the inconvenience of finding a kennel when we needed to leave town, the vexation of house-breaking and the burden of the extra expense.

Eventually Jane and Lo began to speak their own minds about a dog. Naturally, they felt that their desire for a puppy completely overcame the practicality of our reasons not to have one. But we were able to hold our ground until Hollywood and the girls joined forces. At least it seemed suspicious when they so confidently dragged us to see the funny and endearing movie, Beethoven.

As the story goes much to the chagrin of the father who fears that a dog will all but destroy his castle, an adorable St. Bernard puppy strays into the home and hearts of Mom and the kids. The movie depicts how Beethoven also eventually finds his way into Dad's heart. As the children had hoped, its message illustrated to us that we, too, were more concerned about being inconvenienced than allowing them to share the joy of having a pet. Our resolve weakened. Suddenly, we found ourselves in the throes of search-ing for the perfect family dog, with Captain Don leading the pack. Within weeks, a new puppy had made our house its home.

After a year, I had to admit Lucy was a magnificent addition to the Detrich family. She was a purebred Golden Retriever. A book had even been written about her champion grandfather. Lucy's light coloring, massive shoulders, and nearly perfect markings prompted people to remark about her beauty when we'd take her for a walk. But more important to us was her friendly disposition and gentle brown eyes. She would patiently allow Lo to dress her in costumes, sunglasses and t-shirts. She would walk carefully around the family room as visiting babies clung tightly to her tail. She would play soccer in the backyard with whomever was available.

But there was also another side of Lucy. She exemplified protective instincts, particularly for the girls. She stationed herself vigilantly by Jane's side every night as if she knew Jane needed company since her bedroom was at the other end of the house from ours. Once when a stranger walked into the yard towards the house, she pulled Lo away from the window. Another time, when some workmen came to deliver firewood, Lucy, who rarely made a sound, dashed from window to door, snarling and barking the entire time. The next day we began receiving obscene phone calls. We had to wonder if the calls had anything to do with the check I had written for the firewood on which our unlisted phone number was printed. Had Lucy somehow sensed our danger? At any rate, she earned a place of respect and love in our family.

Throughout the years, I continued to remember the seed of hope that I felt God had planted in my heart on the Sunday night prior to Lo's diagnosis. One Saturday afternoon, I found out that in addition to looking after Lo's welfare, He was also looking after the rest of us.

It was one of those exhausting weekends when there were more chores to do than time to do them. Naturally, it was also a time when harmony had been overtaken by discord. I didn't know whether I had awakened on the wrong side of the bed or was just having a tough time getting over one of the migraine headaches I'd been battling more and more frequently. The girls, then eight and twelve, seemed destined to disagree on everything. Don and I, too, had been short with one another. Lucy, sensing the tension, kept to herself.

I was getting more tired and less patient with each petty problem that cropped up — sibling squabbles, throbbing head, housework that would only have to be done again too soon. When Don made the comment that perhaps I might consider watering the houseplants more than once or twice a year, I snapped. "That's it! I don't want to talk to anyone in this house EVER AGAIN!" I was only getting started. My boiling point had been reached and I proceeded to throw a classic temper tantrum screeching hateful remarks at anyone who dared to come within eyesight.

As my anger reached fever pitch, Lucy rounded the corner, carrying a magazine in her mouth. I couldn't help but be a little distracted by the sight. Lucy had never chewed on any of our belongings before. Besides, she had a serious purpose about her that captured my attention. The curiosity of the situation caught me off guard and I fell silent. Slowly, she laid the magazine at my feet, looked up at me with her gentle brown eyes and then turned and walked away.

I looked down to see what my messenger had delivered. It was a copy of Guideposts, an inspirational magazine designed to help people in crisis situations. Lucy had to have retrieved it from a stack of many magazines. I smiled and then laughed at this tiny miracle I had just witnessed. In the midst of our family's mayhem, God, in His infinite wisdom, had used our dog to give me some perspective on our situation. As if sucked up by an invisible tornado, my anger disappeared, taking with it my headache, bad *mood and exhaustion. In fact, no one in our household dared to be anything but pleasant for several days.*

Chapter 31

SOUL
SEARCHING

$\mathcal{P}$rior to Lo's birth, life had
been easy — probably too
easy. I thought the building
blocks of my life were fitting snuggly together, one with the
next, forming a solid foundation for the life of Donald
Detrich. It was merely a matter of balancing roles — that of
husband, father and lawyer. It was fun and rewarding. Then
cystic fibrosis catapulted me into a state of confusion. Life
changed. It became hard — real hard.

At first, I decided I would trust my own instincts as to how
I could best handle raising a child with an incurable disease. If
strength was required, I'd be as strong as I needed to be. If per-
sistence would get it done, I'd draw on sheer determination
and grit. As my dad had said, "My name is Detrich. Give me
the toughest job you've got." Well, I thought, this was a tough
job that I'd been given. But my name was Detrich and I'd fig-

ure out a way to handle it. Period.

And so I handled it . . . and handled it . . . and handled it, until finally the resources my instincts had told me to use proved insufficient for the task. As insomnia, and worry, and work and helping support Terry's efforts to take care of Lo began to zap my energy, I was constantly reminded that my physical, emotional and mental capacities were exhaustible.

I also realized that the priorities I'd established earlier in life seemed misplaced and somehow insignificant in this new world. Position, wealth and business success seemed inconsequential. They couldn't provide the kind of security and peace I needed. I began to question myself, who I was, where I was going and why.

There were symptoms that I was losing my grip. I remember one morning getting ready for work. I had put on a tie, which, along with my overly starched collar, had begun cutting off my circulation. I hated wearing a tie. I then proceeded to try and grasp the incredibly small collar buttons and push them into the even smaller buttonholes. I was in a hurry but the harder I tried, the more the button slipped out of my fingers. My hands were shaking with frustration. Finally, I managed to work the button into the hole when it broke into two small pieces. Suddenly, I was enraged. I groaned, yanked the shirt and tie off, and furiously threw them on the floor. My temper had boiled over because of a button.

"It wasn't the button," was Terry's quiet response.

"What is that supposed to mean?" I glared. But I knew the answer. She was saying it had something to do with my overall state of mind. I knew she was handling our situation better than me. Someone once said "character is who we are in the dark, when no one is there to see us." By that definition, Terry had far more character than I did. Day and night, she seemed to have accepted Lo's illness without bitterness. Part of me resented her for this. Part of me was curious enough about how she did it to listen to her answer.

"You can't handle it alone, Don," she said gently. "You're trying to fix it and you can't."

I knew she was right. I had tried as hard as I could and had succeeded only in becoming bitter, angry and exhausted. "So that makes me a failure," I mumbled dejectedly.

"Not at all. It's just a situation at which you can neither fail nor succeed. You're not the one who's responsible for these circumstances."

"Okay, so I need some answers — some direction. I am going nowhere fast. I know that." The silence was deafening. I could feel Terry's urgency. "I know you're dying to tell me," I said, looking at the floor. "What do you think I should do?"

"I think faith is your answer."

The resentment in me rose again as I heard the word. "You think it's so easy. It's your solution for everything. But I've tried your way, and it doesn't work for me. I can't look at the world through your rose-colored glasses and pretend everything is going to be okay. It's not okay now and it's only going to get worse." This, after all, is the prognosis for cystic fibrosis patients. Lo's health would only deteriorate in years to come.

"I'm not saying the way of faith is easy. In fact, you're going to have to change everything, Don. But I really believe that faith is the only way you're going to find peace."

Somewhere deep within my hurt and anger, I wished I could accept this simple answer. But there was still too much bitterness that had to be confronted. I didn't know it at the time, but Terry had identified at least one of my challenges. I needed to change. The way things were going was not working.

Looking for direction, I became more and more introspective. I went through a long period of self-examination. I read books. I contemplated the flaws that prevented me from letting go of my anger. It was a time of painful honesty. After much contemplation, I realized there was one major aspect of my being which was most responsible for my state. "The problem is pride," I told Terry one night as we walked around the neighborhood. "I can finally admit it. I can't do it by myself. I'm not that good."

"I think you're onto something," Terry said carefully. I knew she was still hesitant to broach the faith subject too directly. So I did it for her.

"We need God the most when we have the least. We need God the most when we have the fewest answers. I think I'm beginning to understand this. It's as if I've been beating my head against the wall. No matter how hard I try, I'll never be good enough, or strong enough, or whatever it takes. It's like He's broken me down until I'm ready to listen to somebody besides myself." I looked over at Terry. She turned her head just slightly, enough for me to see the tears glistening, to see that she was smiling.

I was indeed broken. And from this state of brokenness, I embarked on my journey to find faith in a being, a power greater than me. A faith in God. At that time, I had precious little real faith to draw on. I had gone to a typical Catholic grade school in Chicago. Discipline was the mantra, not self-esteem as it is today. I had stepped over the line on numerous occasions and still had the scars to prove it. My experience with the nuns of my childhood had left me with a faith that was bumped and bruised. In college, my faith turned inward as I explored the Eastern religions. Business success and the materialism of the eighties had left me with almost no faith at all.

I believed in God. It's just that I didn't have any faith in Him. I went through the motions of going to church on Sundays. We prayed each night before the girls went to bed. I wanted to make sure I didn't shirk my duty to teach them about religion. I even read the Bible, beginning to end.

But I was beginning to realize that my faith was just pretend. My relationship with God was purely external. There was nothing personal about it at all. When I prayed, I seldom asked for anything other than to have God change the circumstances that seemed to keep messing up my life. My Bible study was more like a homework assignment — a goal to be accomplished, rather than an attempt to get to know God. No, I decided, this was not the kind of faith that Terry had talked about. It was not the kind of faith that would make a real difference in my life.

I would have to figure it out for myself. Being trained as a lawyer, I tried to think, dissect, analyze and prove faith. I read more. I studied more. I observed and questioned those who I thought had faith. What did they think and why? But despite the fact that I truly wanted to have faith, and that I was working hard at looking for it, I just wasn't able to bridge the mental gap that I sensed separated this elusive concept and me. All I had succeeded in doing was to become even more frustrated.

I was a human being struggling to have a spiritual experience. At the same time, as I observed Lo, she seemed to be a spiritual being enjoying a human experience. While her body was defenseless against the disease, the disease was defenseless against her spirit. There was something to be learned here. I watched her like a hawk.

I soon realized that Lo affected almost everyone who came in contact with her. It didn't matter whether they were friends or strangers. She caused people to embrace the moment in ways they had either forgotten or hadn't previously considered. Lo was happy and excited about life and living. In fact, if I opened a dictionary to look up the definition of joy, I knew I would find a picture of Lo staring at me with those twinkling blue eyes and that full-of-the-dickens smile on her face.

Why? How? She had an incurable disease. I sought the answer to that question during the late lonely hours. I considered, pondered, contemplated, meditated, reflected and mused how she did it. It was of utmost importance to me because I wanted to be that way, too. But it was as if I had a shadowy anchor attached to my psyche, and I was unable to figure out how to disengage from it.

Finally, the answer came as easily as the process had been tortuous. One night, as I walked into Lo's room to tuck her in and kiss her goodnight, I noticed she was way over on one side of her single bed. "Why are you laying on the edge? You could fall off."

I will remember what she said forever. "I have to leave room for Jesus." My throat felt dry, as if the ashes of my dilemma blocked the very air I breathed. Within this image, embedded into the words of my child, was my answer. Lo had not thought her way to faith. She had not rationalized it, excused it, or struggled through it. She had simply accepted it as a gift. She believed that Jesus was by her side to help her through whatever fears and problems she faced. That was how she was able to focus on the wonder and joy of each and every day. And that was how I would have to do the same.

And so I chose to accept this gift of faith. Simple, childlike faith in the goodness and presence of God bridged the gap I had created with all my efforts to manage life and grasp it intellectually. Slowly but surely, I began to accept the idea that God loves us and has a plan for us. No, He doesn't guarantee our lives will be free of adversity, and He doesn't always ensure we escape disaster. And that's okay. Because as Lo had pointed out to me, no matter what we face, He will be there to support us along the way.

Chapter 32

HOME
SCHOOLING

*B*ecause of the time involved to manage her illness, the fulfill-ment of our intention to avoid having cystic fibrosis be the focal point of Lo's life was extreme-ly challenging. It was during her first grade year that we discovered we needed to take more extraordinary measures to maintain our family's ties. Lo had missed so many weeks of school that her initial interest in academics was waning, along with her self-confidence. Jane had suffered from a lack of posi-tive attention from us as well. And Don and I were simply tired, a reality that accompanied the chains of insomniatic distress.

When both my sister and a long-distance friend mentioned they were home schooling their children, my curiosity was tweaked. Would this be a solution for us? I decided to share my idea with Don. "I've been thinking. You know how excited Lo was to go to first grade?" I asked him one wintry night while we relaxed in front of a fire. The girls had gone to bed and we were savoring a few minutes of peace and quiet. I yawned and stretched my feet across well-worn couch cushions while Don munched on chocolate chip cookies at the sofa table behind me. The fire crackled cheerily, the evening news anchors droned in the background. This was the only time of day we could find to mull over strategic directions for our lives.

"Yeah," Don chuckled as he dunked a chocolate chip cookie into a glass of milk. I watched him row the cookie back and forth in the milk for several seconds, then lean over as he pulled it out of the glass and into his mouth.

"Have you noticed she's kind of lost her enthusiasm?"

He paused a moment before reaching for another cookie. "Now that you mention it, I haven't heard her talking about school much lately."

"And you know how we feel like Jane is always in trouble?" I reached over the couch to grab a cookie out of the bag. I pointed the remote control to the TV and turned it off.

With the slightest irritation, Don picked up a fork and fished a soggy cookie out of his glass. "So what are you getting at?"

"What do you think would happen if we taught the girls at home?"

"Home schooling?"

"Yes. I've been talking to Ginny and Cheryl about it. From what they say, the one-on-one attention their children are getting helps them move ahead much faster than they would in the classroom."

"There's no question you'd be able to focus on each student more than a teacher with a room full of kids'd be able to do," Don said thoughtfully as he closed the cookie bag and placed a wadded napkin on his plate. "But how would you know what to teach them? And how can you manage two different grades at *once? Jane'll be in sixth grade next year and Lo in second. I presume you're talking about doing it then."*

I had asked my mentors the same questions. "Families do it all over the country. There are companies that publish curriculums for parents to use. They have teacher's manuals, assignments, tests, everything you need. You order the curriculums through the mail."

"Hmmm. Do you think they'd feel ostracized?" Don asked. "I mean — they'd never see their friends. Would that be one more reason for either of them to end up feeling like the odd man out?"

"I worry about that, too," I admitted. "But I worry more that the kids feel insecure about our family. Our situation is so ridiculous. You and I are tired and distracted by CF. Lo's been sick more than well. We spend more time correcting Jane than complimenting her. Maybe if we home-schooled, we could have some fun rather than simply react to one disaster after another."

"Well, that'd be different," Don laughed, adding, "and I like different — not trying to do exactly what everyone else does. Why don't you talk to Sister Mary Clare and see what she thinks? I don't want to take the girls out of Monte Cassino if it's going to burn any bridges."

"I agree. If it doesn't work out, I would hope they'd let us back in." I made a mental note to contact the well-respected Benedictine nun who ran our school.

Don pushed his chair back and carried his plate to the kitchen. He crossed the den floor to the fireplace, lifted the stoker off the side of the mantle, and pushed the cinders back away from the screen. "How long do you think we'd do this home schooling anyway?" he finally said.

I stood up and walked over to lower the blinds for the night. A bitter wind blew the highest limbs of a huge oak tree back and forth, sending a light show to the patio from the bulb at the top of a telephone pole in the corner of the yard. The tree had weathered years of wind, rain and storms. It had grown tall and strong through the changing seasons. Change was inevitable, I thought. And with change came risk. What would we risk by taking the girls out of school, I wondered. Were my concerns really worth the effort that I would no doubt have to make?

"I don't think I'd want to commit for more than a year," I said aloud. "I have a feeling it's going to take up every bit of extra time I have. I don't know if I could do it any longer. But maybe a year will enable the girls to regain some level of security that they have a home and a family and parents who care more about them than a disease or lack of a good night's sleep."

Fortunately, Sister Mary Clare was completely supportive of the idea. She, too, had a sister who had home-schooled her children. "We'll be here if you need us," she assured me. "We'll just keep Jane on her regular basketball team so she can maintain her friendships with her schoolmates. We can also give you our curriculum booklet to use as a guide." Don and I were both extremely grateful that she appreciated our motivation was not to buck a perfectly good system but to serve purposes unique to our family's situation.

The rest of the spring and summer I evaluated curriculums and made phone calls to experienced home-schooling families, gathering as much information as I could. Though a little bit tentative, the girls began to get more and more excited about the idea, particularly when Don and I informed them that the first activity planned would be a vacation at the beach.

"Wow!" they both shouted. "We like this kind of school."

At the end of the summer when their friends headed to Monte Cassino, we took off for the Deep South, stopping at an antebellum mansion to spend a night in four-poster beds restored to their original beauty. We toured Civil War battlefields, crouch-

ing behind cannons, walking around the grassy knolls where bullet casings were still found on a regular basis. We read bills of sale in County Courthouse museums that were used to trade slaves in Mississippi. Along the way, we talked about directions, geography, history and economics. All four of us learned far more than we could have hoped. Days later, we found ourselves nearly threatened by Hurricane Andrew, one of the strongest hurricanes to hit the Florida coastline in the century. Though we escaped its path, the girls drew an appreciation of meteorology as they watched buildings being boarded up for protection against the winds. They learned about the influence of tides as they enjoyed the high surf of the Gulf of Mexico. As we crossed each border, we pulled off the road to pose for a family picture next to the state's welcome sign. These photos recorded the beginning of one of the most memorable years our family ever experienced.

Two weeks later, our academic program began in earnest back at home. Our school day started around nine o'clock in the morning and was over by lunchtime. We covered all the basic subjects that both children would have had in regular school. We literally sailed through the material I had ordered, finishing a semester's worth of work in half the time it would normally have taken.

It had been years since I'd had the pleasure of watching Jane devour new concepts. I'd almost forgotten how she had so easily put together twenty piece puzzles at age one. I had also forgotten how astonished I'd been when at four, she had asked me why the President of the United States didn't go to the Middle East to resolve the hostage crisis. The intervening years of chronic illness and its consequences had left little time for us to help Jane develop her remarkable gifts. Home schooling afforded us the opportunity to again appreciate the value of her inquisitive personality.

It also enabled us to simply share our enthusiasm for

learning as we enjoyed one another's company. "Momma, will you read to me?" *Jane said one afternoon.*

"Sure, honey. After lunch. How about Maniac McGee?"

"Yeah, that's funny," *Jane smiled.* "I'll go find it for you."

I picked up our lunch dishes and put away our lessons for the day. Then we situated ourselves on the couch in the den. Jane cuddled up next to me. Lost in the story of a young boy's school experiences, we read chapter after chapter, laughing and crying.

"I love to do this," *Jane smiled sleepily after we'd finished the book. I put it down and pulled her onto my lap. It didn't matter that she was in the sixth grade. It felt so good to hold this child of mine, to spend time with her, to forget about the disease that so often seemed to create distance between us. Home-schooling allowed me to at least occasionally offer Jane my undivided attention and affection.*

Don, too, participated in our home-schooling adventures. When weather permitted, he led the girls in physical education activities after work. Stretching exercises preceded a jog around the neighborhood. "Find your stride, Jane. Look strong," *he'd shout encouraging remarks.* "You can go the distance, Lo." *The distance gradually grew, resulting in thirty- to forty-five-minute runs which spanned two to three miles.*

By October, Lo was searching for new ways to use her free time in the afternoons. "Mommy, I'd like to plan a carnival," *she announced one crisp autumn morning.*

"What do you mean — a carnival? You mean with your stuffed animals?" *I asked, assuming she was envisioning the furry friends who populated her imaginary classrooms or staffed her pretend offices.*

"No, I mean a real carnival with real people who come to the house."

"Oh, is that so," *I raised my eyebrows.* "Well, I'll tell you what, Lo. If you want to do something that big, then you're going to have to come up with a plan. You need a budget of how much money this activity's going to cost, what supplies you'll need, when it will be held, who you will invite. And Daddy and I need to approve your plan before you launch into it."

"Sounds good to me," Lo accepted the request cheerfully. I had hoped my demands would cause her idea to fizzle out as she began to factor in the time and effort a carnival would take. I forgot that to my youngest daughter, planning was as much fun as executing. For the next two days, Lo was constantly writing, drawing, adding and subtracting. At least, I thought, she was applying every skill she'd been learning. Every now and then, she would giggle, and announce, "Mommy, this is so much fun!"

My own attitude began to change as I watched the determination with which she pursued her plan.

"When would you like to hear about my carnival?" she finally asked.

"Well, I guess now's as good a time as any," I said.

"Great! Let's sit at the kitchen table." We'd had a butcher-block table custom-made for the corner of our kitchen two years before. It had since become the center of many activities, including home schooling, mealtime, games and conversation.

"What have you cooked up, little girl?"

Lo launched into a series of sketches and lists. She had taken her imaginary playtimes to a whole new level. "I can dress up in my clown costume, and sell tickets around the neighborhood," she began. "We'll have games and rides and a cake walk. It'll be a great way for the neighbors to get together and the kids will love it."

"It's a great idea, honey, but it sounds pretty involved," I said as I began to assume the significance of my part of the effort. Lo read my mind. "Don't worry, Mom. I'll take care of everything.

I've made a budget, just like you asked. We'll have it a week from Saturday in the afternoon when nothing else is going on." Lo grinned up at me, her eyes flashing with excitement. My resistance vanished.

"Well, let's talk to Daddy tonight," I said, knowing the event was all but scheduled.

"Oh, Mommy, you're the best!" Pulling me down, she pressed her cheek tightly against mine.

With Don's blessing, Lo spent her afternoons for the next two weeks directing her advertising campaign, running errands and baking cookies. The neighbors were apparently busy as well. At one o'clock in the afternoon on the day of the carnival, men, women and children came strolling over with freshly baked cakes for the cakewalk. They also brought plenty of coins for chances to win back the goods they'd made. Children jumped on the trampoline in the backyard; adults sipped on lemonade and munched cookies. Lo, the clown, buzzed around the yard, meeting and greeting one and all. Don, Jane and I provided background support.

That evening, we swept up the garage and emptied the trash from the concessions. "I'm exhausted, but you know what? That was a blast," I said, surprising myself. "How does she get us to do this stuff?"

"She worked harder than anybody," Don said, slipping a twist tie onto a garbage bag and swinging it over his shoulder. "She made sure every single person had a great time. She has more initiative and drive than anybody I've ever seen."

"Maybe this is proof that home schooling was a good idea," I said, folding a card table and leaning it against the wall. "We couldn't have done this if the girls hadn't been home during the afternoons. It's been a learning project."

"I think you're right, Terry. But let's hope Lo doesn't dream up any more projects until after Christmas. I don't think the home school staff can take any more till then."

When the school year came to an end, we knew it was time to re-enter the mainstream of institutional education. True to her word, Sister Mary Clare and the faculty at Monte Cassino welcomed us back with open arms, as did the girls' classmates. Many people may have questioned our decision to home school, in light of the time we were already spending on Lo's care. But we wouldn't trade that year for anything. Never again were we just Mom, Dad, and kids. Our year of home schooling proved to be one in which we grew to admire one another's strengths and talents as individuals with unique ideas and aspirations.

Chapter 33

ALTERNATIVES

So there we were, in many respects, the average American family — Mom, Dad, two kids and a dog. To the casual observer, nothing was amiss. We went to work, to school. We had season tickets to the University of Tulsa football and basketball games. We went to church. We continued to work on raising funds for CF. We had successfully continued to go through the motions of daily life for the better part of a decade. Even if someone knew we had a child with a life-threatening disease, Lo always seemed so happy and energetic that it was hard for many people to believe anything was wrong with her. But we knew it all too well. We knew it as we watched Lo's pulmonary function levels decrease, the computerized graphs depicting the peaks and flows of her respiratory system taking on the paths of gradual obstruction and deterioration. We knew something was amiss as the cumulative signs of insomnia showed up in Terry's and my alarming lack of short-term memory, the burning sensation of our red-rimmed eyes, the aching joints and muscle spasms in our backs, the daily headaches, the premature lines in our faces. We knew it when we dropped Jane off at school — when she would scarcely say good-by, rather just get out of the car and walk away. The moments of affection were too often offset by those of contention. Ten years of chronic illness, lack of sleep and distress had taken a toll on each of us, a toll that threatened to bring total destruction unless we pursued new paths.

One evening I leaned back in my recliner, randomly clicking the remote. Lo was doing a breathing treatment in her room. Jane was studying. Terry sat on the couch next to me, a stack of magazines piled up by her side. "Can't you ever relax?" I asked, finally settling on the Monday night football game. "I don't think I've ever seen you sit down on that couch without pens and papers or books and magazines. Why don't you let it go and just watch TV?"

"This is how I relax," she retorted. Several minutes went by as I semi-watched the Dallas Cowboys score a touchdown.

"Guess what I did this afternoon?" Terry suddenly announced.

"What?" I said.

"I was driving around trying to get some errands run. I had a splitting headache. I'd taken aspirin, and the pills the doctor gave me. Nothing was helping. I had to do something. So, I stopped at a convenience store and looked in the yellow pages for a masseuse."

"You got a massage?" I asked. "Good for you."

"I went to a school where they train people and the instructor had some time. He worked on me for an hour."

"Did it help your head?"

"Yes, actually it did. But that's not even the important part.

The guy told me there was a man in town that we should go see. He practices homoeopathy."

"What's homoeopathy?"

"It's one of the alternative medicine practices that's becoming more and more popular."

"Alternative medicine?"

"Yes. There are homoeopaths, naturopaths, herbalists, and a host of other kinds of medical specialists that people go see when their regular doctors can't help them."

"You mean when you have things like just being tired?" I sighed.

"Exactly," Terry said. "What have we got to lose, Don? We're tired all the time. It's embarrassing. We're not old enough to be falling apart. And we've been to doctors. Several of them. They didn't seem to have any magic potions for us."

"Yeah, but what do we know about this guy?"

"Not much," Terry admitted.

I had reached a state of desperation. I couldn't see any reason not to pursue a new route to a decent night's sleep, even if it might turn out to be another dead end. "I'm ready to try anything," I said. "Set it up. It's not like we have to do anything if we don't want to."

On Saturday morning, we left the girls at home and drove over to an address in an older neighborhood. It was a two-story stone house, normal-looking enough, we decided. Terry and I weren't quite sure what we were getting into but curiosity was a powerful incentive at that point. We walked up to the front door and rang the bell. A hand-written note was taped on the mailbox. It requested that guests not wear perfume or other strong scents inside.

A minute later the door opened. "Come in," a man greeted us. "I'm Tim." He was about six feet tall and thin, neatly dressed in khaki slacks, a white cotton polo shirt and sandals. He shook our hands and smiled, pointing in the direction of a room toward the back of the house. "This is where we'll meet," he said. The house was attractively furnished, nothing extraordinarily bizarre or unique, I thought. So far, at least I didn't feel like we had completely gone off the deep end.

We entered a room, painted white, with hardwood floors, bookcases lining one wall, a large picture window centering another. A massage table was set up in the middle of the room. Two director's chairs and an end table offered seating. A quiet humming sound came from an air cleaner stationed in a corner. "You guys are welcome to sit down," Tim motioned towards the chairs. "I'll sit on the floor. Would you like a glass of water?"

"Sure," we both accepted his offer. We could hear the sound of a baby's voice through the wall behind me. "You have a little one?" I asked as he handed us glasses.

"We have a six-month old daughter," Tim said. "She's a doll. I'd love to introduce her to you later." He took off his sandals and sat down, tailor fashioned in stocking feet. "So, what brings you two here?" he asked.

We told him that we had been to an assortment of doctors for a variety of ailments. Though they were all sympathetic to our plight, none of them had been able to help our insomnia effectively, which we thought was our biggest problem. We asked him where he had been trained and exactly what it was he did for people.

"I got into this field because of my own illness several years ago," he started. "I had gotten to the point where I was bedridden. I couldn't work; I couldn't face the day. I had no energy or enthusiasm. I believe that I had what has been commonly called chronic fatigue syndrome. There was no treatment or cure. Frankly," he stopped to laugh, "there was never a definitive diagnosis except for mine."

"But I started reading about other people who had these mysterious bouts of illness with no known cause or solution. I changed the way I ate, the kind of water I drank and the amount. I studied about supplements and began taking the ones I felt could help me. I eventually came upon a German homoeopathist who had developed a system to evaluate people's reactions to toxins and then to treat them. I went over to Germany and ended up working with him for several months. In the meantime, I got better. When I came back, I decided I wanted to help other people get better, too. So here I am."

Then Tim asked us about our family situation, what incidents we'd been through that had caused stress, what our responses had been. Throughout our session, he took notes. Finally, he said, "I think I can help you." He looked at our eyes, our hands, and our feet. He explained that different parts of our bodies react to stress and that often the evidence shows up externally. He explained that our level of health, or well-being, depends upon how various levels of our needs are met, from those rudimentary needs like air and water all the way up to the highest levels of being that are more oriented to self-actualization.

"You all have been through a lot," he sympathized. "Your experience has left you nearly defenseless against toxins. It's no wonder you're always exhausted. You're both out of balance. That's what homeopathy is all about. Getting the body back to its natural balance."

"How do we go about doing that?" I asked.

"We evaluate how you respond to various toxins and then we put you on an individualized program of supplements. As you get better, the supplements change."

"Is it expensive?" Terry asked.

Tim smiled. "I guess that all depends on how you look at it. They are not nearly as expensive as the medical bills you have probably been paying." He then asked us about our diets and recommended some rather drastic changes, including the elimination of processed foods, such as sugary desserts, and the addition of more fiber.

Tim explained that our adrenal glands were designed to release chemicals in times of extreme stress — the fight or flight response. After using a magnetic device to monitor our reactions to a number of different liquids in tiny bottles, he concluded our adrenals had been working overtime — since Lo's birth. According to Tim's analysis, they were completely depleted. He wrote out a list of vitamins, cellular salts, and minerals that he wanted each of us to take. The supplements he prescribed were distinctly different for each of us, based on his assessment of our bodies' uniquenesses. The total bill for the supplements and consultation was two hundred dollars. We'd been there for nearly three hours.

I had to admit that much of what Tim said made sense. I knew that I was quite simply running on fumes. I didn't know where else to turn. I decided that I would commit myself to Tim's methodology and see how much difference it could make.

I began going to the office with my pockets full of pills to swallow and liquids to be taken sublingually, dissolved under the tongue. I ordered bottled water to be installed in our firm's kitchen. I eliminated my lifelong habit of eating cookies and milk at night. I even went to a series of cooking classes with Terry to learn about macrobiotic eating, a kind of healing art practiced by the Japanese. I started exercising during the noon hour, gradually at first, as Tim said my condition was too run-down to push myself physically.

Maybe I was just glad to be doing something different, but I looked forward to my sessions with Tim. Each time he would pull out his odd assortment of little bottles and magnetic equipment and tell me how I needed to adapt my diet or supplemental program. During the sessions he would also share with me information he'd read over the years. I began to realize how oriented to Western medicine I had always been. There was a whole other approach to healing on the other side of the Pacific Ocean. It had been practiced for thousands of years by billions of people. Suddenly, everywhere Terry and I looked there were articles being published about these alternatives for health care, acupuncture, acupressure, massage, homeopathy, and dozens more methods of helping people who were on a quest for well-being.

After several months, I began to sense that I was regaining a certain amount of strength and energy. Occasionally, I would even get a few more hours of sleep at night. If I had a reversal, I would go see Tim and he would analyze my toxin levels, or perform acupuncture.

Shortly before Christmas, my friend from high school, Hannah Rosenthal, who now lived in Madison, Wisconsin, reminded me that she had run into a Korean doctor several years before who was successfully treating two children with cystic fibrosis in Madison. This doctor traveled to Madison several times each year from Dallas. She knew we were going to Dallas for the holidays. "Why don't you and Terry think about taking Lo to see Dr. Choe?" she asked. "He has treated these two boys as well as hundreds of other people up here. He's even treated me for some back problems. I think he's wonderful."

After our success with Tim and our newly acquired open-mindedness to alternative medicine, we decided to pay the doctor a visit with Lo. He invited us to come to his house on Christmas Eve morning. Terry and I, Lo, my dad and brother, Jeff, all piled in the car. Curiosity ruled again.

"Hello," the slightly built oriental man welcomed us. His house was in an affluent area of old Dallas. It was large and comfortable. Tapestries and paintings were hung about the huge living room. Some were of oriental scenes or flowers, others were religious — scenes of Christ speaking to the disciples. It was an eclectic combination. "Please come," he pointed to a room adjacent to the living room. Like Tim, he wore simple clothing, sandals with stockings. The floor in the room was hardwood, covered by an area mat. A large picture window allowed the sun to bathe the room in warm light. He looked at Lo with a gentle smile. "Now, you lie here. On stomach, please." He motioned to the mat and sat down at one end of it, tailor-fashioned. "Please put your head here," he placed a paper towel on the mat.

The rest of us sat alongside the mat and watched. Dr. Choe pressed on the upper part of Lo's spine with his thumbs, leaving them there for several minutes. Then he moved just slightly down and did the same thing. Within a short while, Lo fell sound asleep. A look of total calm came over her face. Dr. Choe smiled, barely nodding his head as if in approval.

As we watched him move down her spine, then over to her shoulders and arms, we began to ask questions about his practice. He had spent his lifetime traveling all over the world. He had worked on people of great and small means. People like us and people like Katherine Hepburn. He had even worked on the Pope. He had spent fifteen years being trained in the technique he called Sugi. He believed the treatments he gave people could help them with almost any ailment they had.

"What exactly is happening when you do whatever it is that you're doing?" I finally asked him.

"The little girl is healing herself," Dr. Choe smiled. "Energy in her body is blocked. This causes problems — congestion. When we press, it helps her eliminate the blockage and restore balance."

"Don't you get tired after a while?" Terry asked.

"Never gets tired. Treatments give me energy, too."

Suddenly, Dr. Choe stood up and said, "Now I walk on little girl's back. With an air of total confidence and gentleness, he placed one foot and then the other on Lo's back. He leaned almost imperceptibly from one side to the other, and then took small steps up and down. After several minutes, he stepped off and leaned down. "Roll over, please," he spoke softly to Lo, helping her turn over.

He worked on her for an hour or more and then said, "Let her sleep. Now — you." He pointed to Terry. Terry had benefited from Tim's supplements but her headaches had continued unabated. She was more than willing to be the next subject. Again, within minutes, she was fast asleep. After another hour, Dr. Choe was finished. "You come back tomorrow," he announced matter-of-factly.

"But it's Christmas," I said.

"Is okay. Christmas is good time to feel good," he grinned. "Better you come every day you are here."

Lo sat up and smiled at the little man. "I feel great!" she exclaimed. "Thank you, Dr. Choe."

"I can't believe it but my headache is gone," Terry said. "That's amazing."

Needless to say, we returned the next day and the day after that. I had to go back to Tulsa but the girls stayed on until New Year's Eve. At the time he finished her treatments, Dr. Choe declared, "Now, she will grow."

I can't say that I truly understand the alternative healing arts. I didn't end up rejecting the western arts that I had been exposed to for my entire life. But, mysterious as it may sound, Lo did enter a growth spurt shortly after her treatments. She gained both weight and height and has maintained a normal size for her age ever since. Terry's headaches disappeared for months as well.

We were convinced enough about Dr. Choe's technique to invite him to stay at our house that summer and treat nearly a hundred friends and acquaintances. We witnessed several people respond dramatically. One woman came in with bruises from her ankle to her knee on crutches, barely able to walk. She left with the bruises almost gone and walked unaided with only a slight limp. This was after two hours of Dr. Choe's pressing actions. Another woman who had experienced severe back problems for years was able to restart her walking program after Dr. Choe's help. On an occasion, we continue to see Dr. Choe when he comes to town. If insurance covered this kind of treatment, we would regularly use it.

We can't explain why these alternative medical treatments work but our experiences with them clearly demonstrated to us that they are well worth pursuing. From our layperson's perspective we witnessed enough success to believe that another world of knowledge lies beyond the boundaries of traditional Western medicine.

Chapter 34

LO'S NEWS

"**H**ey, Lo! You need to come in for a breathing treatment," I yelled out the back door. The sound of children's laughter rang out in the heat of a June afternoon. Lucy languished on the ground in the middle of the yard, a soccer ball placed strategically at her two front paws, her eyes focused hopefully on a young boy and girl jumping on a trampoline.

"Okay, Mom, we'll be there in a sec," Lo answered as she and her friend, Blake, took turns springing the other one higher and higher. Blake and his family had moved in around the corner from us the previous fall. Lo and Blake were the same age, and similarly sized, though they were a grade apart in school. They had struck up a friendship that provided constant companionship in the afternoons and on vacation days.

I watched them climb off the trampoline and pull on their tennis shoes. As they ran toward the house, Blake kicked the soccer ball over Lucy's head. Lucy immediately bounded over to retrieve it. "Look at her go," Blake laughed. "She'd be the best player on our team."

"You want to play Nintendo while I do my treatment?" Lo asked.

Kicking the ball across the yard again, Blake said, "Sure. I just got a new game last night. It's awesome. I'll go home and get it." Ten minutes later, the two were intently swapping strategies on their latest video challenges, giggling hilariously as one or the other gained access to higher levels of play.

"Man, I can't believe I did that again," Blake grumbled good-naturedly, handing the controller over to Lo.

"Well, don't worry about it. My turn probably won't last very long," Lo consoled him.

I smiled gratefully as I realized the number of supportive children, like Blake, who were willing to wait with Lo as she inhaled the various medications she took hour after hour of every day. They never complained about keeping her company. They could have stayed outside and played, or gone home. But usually they wanted to hang around, watch and figure out something to do during Lo's treatments. In fact, many were fascinated by all the things she 'got' to do.

"Is it done?" I stuck my head around the corner after a half hour had gone by.

"I think so," Lo answered, pulling the mouthpiece out and shaking the nebulizer to see if any liquid remained in its reservoir. As she'd grown older, she was able to control her breathing better, so we had graduated from masks to devices she held in her mouth. This enabled her to breathe more medication into her lungs and allowed less to escape into the air.

"Let's do some boomps for a while now," I suggested, thinking that an abbreviated session would be sufficient in light of the exercise she'd had jumping on the trampoline.

She lay on her stomach over a pillow on the floor. I began clapping her back and shoulders rhythmically for several minutes. "You get to do that every day?" Blake asked Lo. He sat on the floor a few feet away, leaning on an ottoman, his arms criss-crossed over bent knees. "That looks like it would feel good."

"Yeah, Blake," Lo huffed. "It does for about the first minute. Then the rest of the time it kind of hurts."

"Would you like to try it for a second?" I offered. "That way you can see for yourself what it feels like."

"Okay," Blake agreed. Lo rolled off the pillow to make room for him. "Like this?" Blake situated himself as he remembered Lo doing.

"That's perfect," I said and began clapping on his back. "Now breathe deeply."

"Hey, that tickles." Blake laughed.

"Just wait another minute," Lo suggested, lying on the floor next to me.

"I can't lie this way. I can't see the TV."

"Yeah, I know. I can't either half the time."

"You have to do that every single day?" Out of the mouths of babes, I thought.

"Two times every single day," I said, giving him a hand to sit back up.

"Gees, Lo." Blake's wide-eyed gaze revealed a newfound insight into the world of chronic illness. "I guess that's not as much fun as it looks."

"Oh well," she shrugged. "Want to go back outside now?"

"Yeah, let's go ride bikes."

"Bye, Mom."

As the summer wore on, Blake's commitments to baseball and tennis afforded Lo additional time alone to formulate her latest ideas. One morning she entered my bedroom with a piece of *paper in her hand. "Can we go to Kinko's?" she asked.*

"What for?"

"I'm starting a neighborhood newspaper. I've written the first edition. Would you like one?"

"What's that going to cost me, Lo?"

"Only twenty-five cents."

"Well, I guess I can afford that."

"I'm going to write an edition every week, so if you want to save money you can buy a whole subscription."

"A salesman at heart," I laughed. "I'll take one."

"As soon as I'm finished, I'll deliver it to you."

By the time Lo had gone up and down our block she had a list of customers. "I can pay for copying the newspaper with part of the money I collect for subscriptions," she said.

"That's good thinking, Lo. You're a real entrepreneur."

"What's does that mean?"

"You turn good ideas into businesses that make money."

"I like that," she decided instantly. "I always have ideas. I like business. And it's fun to make money."

Lo's first newspaper was handwritten and only a few sentences long. However, the idea spread around the neighborhood, prompting interest. She decided to offer her customers an expanded edition and give her paper a name. Ranch Acres News was printed first on our home computer. It included both a weather report filled with bullets such as: 'rain — maybe'; and 'thunder — probably not'; and graphics she pulled out of a clip art file. In the next edition, she added, "Tip of the Day" — which was a subtle 'Mow Your Lawn,' and an interview of one of the neighborhood's elder statesmen.

When she decided to incorporate contests for prizes, the phone started ringing. "I have the answer to the riddle in Lo's Times." (The paper seemed to change names quite frequently.)

"The question was 'What's black and white and read all over?' I think it's the newspaper."

"You are absolutely correct," I congratulated the caller.

"Is Lo going to deliver the free liter of cola or are you?" the caller chuckled.

Other neighbors requested additional copies to send to relatives out-of-town. "We really look forward to each issue," one woman said. "We've been sharing them over the phone with my sister. She'd like a copy of her own."

Occasionally, illness postponed an issue, although the publisher eventually made good on her commitment. Ultimately, she tired of the effort and closed the operation down. Her next venture would prove to be her greatest one. Meanwhile, Lo Detrich, entrepreneur extraordinaire, added another enterprise to the list of successful ventures.

Chapter 35

PHOENIX
VISIONS

O n the proverbial heels of the discovery of the gene, a new med-cation was rushed through research and development for CF patients. Now we were finally able to connect our fundraising efforts to a result that would help Lo directly. The drug was called Pulmozyme. A researcher named Steven Shak, whose work had been previously supported by the National Institutes of Health and the Cystic Fibrosis Foundation, identified the basic ingredient of the drug. The Genentech Corporation funded the clinical phases of testing for the product. We followed the progress of Pulmozyme and its lightning-fast pace through the Food and Drug Administration's approval process. Whereas the average cycle for a drug to be approved for use was over a decade, Pulmozyme received the nod in less than five years. In the winter of 1995, it became the first new drug approved for the treatment of CF symptoms in twenty years. Though it didn't promise to reverse, or even stop the progress of the disease, it did appear to offer a way to break up some of the debris that clogged the lungs of patients enabling them to breathe more easily. Researchers hoped that Pulmozyme would allow patients to live more comfortably with cystic fibrosis until science came up with a treatment or control for the root cause of the disease.

On the first Saturday of January, Pati Richardson, still our faithful home care nurse, called to say that she had the drug at her office and wanted to deliver it to our house. Lo, now nine years old, would get to be the first official patient in the area to receive a breathing treatment with Pulmozyme. All four of us were waiting at the front door when Pati pulled up.

"This is it!" Pati exclaimed, pulling a small box out of her car. "I am so excited I can't believe it."

"We're making history today," I said.

"Are you ready, Lo?"

"I'm ready," Lo smiled.

We walked into the kitchen and Pati handed Terry a plastic bag. "This is the new nebulizer you have to use. It's designed to create much finer particles that can penetrate the airways more effectively than older nebulizers could. You can't put anything else in it or it will negate the effect of Pulmozyme. And this — is Pulmozyme. She pulled out a foil envelope. She cut an opening in the top and removed a small ampoule of medication. "This stuff is like liquid gold. It costs almost thirty dollars a dose."

We all watched Pati twist the top off of the ampoule and pour it into the reservoir of the nebulizer. It would not have filled a tablespoon but we were anxious to see what a difference it would make to Lo's condition.

"Cameras ready?" Pati asked, handing Lo the nebulizer.

"I'm going to save the ampoule for posterity's sake," Terry laughed, placing it in a plastic bag she had labeled 'First Pulmozyme Dose.'

"Lo, just breathe this in like you would any other medicine," Pati counseled.

Lo positioned the mouthpiece and flicked on the machine. We all sat and waited expectantly.

"Notice anything?" I asked her hopefully.

"I can't tell yet, Daddy." After the treatment was finished, we sat around and watched Lo for a few minutes. "It feels okay," she decided. "Can I go play now?"

We were a little disappointed but didn't know if it was reasonable to expect any immediate reactions. "Sure. Have fun."

The drug was to be taken only once a day. We waited until Sunday morning for dose number two. An hour after Lo's second dose, Terry and I sat in the kitchen reading the newspaper. Suddenly, Lo came running in with a huge smile on her face. "Guess what?" she beamed. "I really can tell a difference. I wasn't sure yesterday but today I can feel it in my lungs. Now I know how you all feel when you breathe. It's great!"

We were ecstatic to think that the medicine made even the slightest bit of difference. Monday, more objective results confirmed Lo's evaluation when Terry took her in to Dr. Kramer's for a pulmonary function test. Lo's scores were far higher than normal.

"Marvelous!" Dr. Kramer responded with enthusiasm. "However," he cautioned, "this is probably temporary. After the initial doses, the scores tend to go down. Our observation is that eventually they find a new level, better than before the drug. Our hope is that Pulmozyme will help her stay healthier in the long run."

Lo's experience with Pulmozyme ended up following along the same lines as the patients who had participated in the clinical testing. Her high scores were followed within weeks by a downturn. She contracted pneumonia shortly after that and ended up on intravenous therapy for three weeks. But by summertime, her pulmonary function rates had evened out, and thankfully, they were a little higher than they had been prior to the drug, giving us hope that the promise of the drug would be realized.

Meanwhile, our efforts to raise funds continued unabated, fueled by the reality of progress attributed to Pulmozyme. In between her treatments and social activities, Lo served as Poster Child and Goodwill Ambassador for the Sooner Chapter of the CF Foundation. Terry and I assisted where we could as board members, committee members and volunteers for the chapter's events.

Many who had offered their help on our initial All Sports Ball still committed their efforts on a regular basis. A friend since college days, Bill Thomas had chaired a golf tournament that was being copied around the country. The All Sports Ball's success, as well, was a showcase of ideas for events in other chapters. Kathleen Hilti had continued to pursue sources of major contributions around the country and had become involved in the international foundation's activities. She and her husband, Markus, had opened their home to us countless times for magnificent parties benefiting CF.

On all fronts, it seemed for the first time that we were getting a new perspective on our situation — a perspective that provided a certain amount of encouragement. First, it appeared that we were gaining momentum in the race for a cure for cystic fibrosis. The gene had been discovered. All indications were that gene therapy was just around the corner.

Second, our family was still together. Jane was in her last year of middle school, Lo, in the fourth grade, Terry and I still married. Somehow our little family appeared to have weathered the storm for a decade.

So it was perfect timing, really, that we received an invitation to speak at a convention of five hundred medical professionals in Phoenix in February of 1995. Pati, our nurse, had recommended us to represent the patients and caregivers served by her corporation. "We want to know who our customers are," she explained. "We want to know what it's like to have someone in the family with chronic illness — from your point of view. We want to know if you think we're doing a good job." We didn't know that the opportunity to share our perspective with others would mark another turning point in our lives.

Coram Healthcare Corporation, Pati's company, flew all four of us out to Phoenix for the five-day convention. We were given beautiful accommodations in the hotel where the convention was held. We were invited to attend all of the events that were part of the entertainment portion of the meeting. The company executives said that our presence helped keep the employees' focus on Coram's reason for being. Our keynote address fell on the last day of the formal sessions.

Terry and I discussed ahead of time what topics each of us would handle. We decided that I would speak first. I would try to help the audience picture life in our house — what it was like to be the father of a critically ill child, how I dealt with issues such as the financial pressure of paying for a catastrophic disease, how cystic fibrosis impacted our family as a whole. I would try and help them better understand the meaning of the term chronic illness. Terry would then cover Lo's diagnosis, her day-to-day regimen, our expectations of medical professionals and our opinions of Coram's care.

As we spoke, both Terry and I became acutely aware of the audience's attentiveness to our presentation. For the first time, we sensed that the experience we had gained over the past decade appeared to have inestimable value for these doctors, nurses, administrators, technicians and executives. To top it off, after we were finished, Lo decided she had a few words to add, both as a tribute to Pati, her faithful nurse, and to all who were helping her fight her disease. Her words spoke volumes, providing a child's view of her illness and of the tremendous impact of others' efforts on her behalf.

She told about a stuffed animal Pati had given her years before and how this simple gesture of kindness engendered trust and helped diffuse the fearful situation of enduring repeated insertions of needles. "I still have Lambchop and sometimes I still get IVs but I don't cry anymore. I remember the days when it snows and Pati comes and gives me an IV and then Mom will have to go and get something and we'll stay home and play Monopoly. I've always really liked Pati and she's never really tried to hurt me."

In closing, Lo offered a profound acknowledgement of her situation, creating a poignant vision for all of the confluence of joy and sorrow in living with a deadly disease. She said with a smile as bright as the Phoenix sunshine, "Hopefully, one day maybe there will be a cure for CF. I hope I'm still alive when that day does come. I just want to say thank you, all of you, for being here every step of the way for all your patients and all of us. Thank you."

There were five hundred medical professionals in the audience that day. In recognition of Phoenix's reputation as being in the valley of the sun, sunglasses had been placed on each chair as a memento. From our vantage point on the stage, we watched five hundred pairs of teary eyes being covered with sunglasses almost in unison.

For the next thirty-six hours, members of Coram's staff approached us constantly, each one wanting additional information on the topics we had covered. "You should write a book," several people suggested. "You could help all of us better understand how we need to respond to people in your situation. You could help others like yourselves understand what they are going through. You could just help us know how to deal with adversity."

I can't remember at exactly what point Terry and I looked at one another and smiled. We had discussed years before how nice it would be to have a book that would give some insights into what we were facing. Now, the years had given us a vast amount of experience that we could draw from to tell our story. Not that we purported to be experts or that we had managed to handle our circumstances particularly well. But the fact that others could learn from our story, our successes and our failures, elated us. Just as raising funds for a cure had provided us with hope, writing a book might enable us to create something of value out of our lives, something that might help others avoid pitfalls, or offer them an element of empathy, the assurance that they were not alone.

The vision that came out of Phoenix was clear. We would write a book. This book.

Chapter 36

GREAT STRIDES

I sighed. Two pocket folders, one yellow, the other blue, lay open in front of me. The yellow one included all the medical bills I needed to file for the month. There were a couple invoices each for Don and me, none for Jane and a large stack for Lo. The blue folder contained the explanations of benefits already paid out for the year. Don's, Jane's and mine fit more than comfortably in the pocket on the left side. It would only take a few months before Lo's would barely fit in the right. I could easily look at the bottom of these benefit forms to see the current balance remaining on Lo's million-dollar cap. Increasing medical costs drove the average annual benefits paid skyward. With Lo nearing her tenth birthday, her balance was being depleted at a rate of about $75,000 a year.

Tracking insurance claims was a forbidding task. I had become intimately familiar with industry terms used by both physicians and the insurance companies. I was accustomed to matching dates of service with services provided, comparing fees with those charged on previous dates and at least attempting to reconcile whether or not we were paying a fair price for the reasonable and customary fees deemed allowable by our insurance carrier.

I was still rather proud of myself for having discovered some years previously, an overcharge of several thousand dollars for one three-month prescription of an antibiotic. The drug was expensive, in part because the kind of delivery system it required was fairly new. It was given via inhalation. The generic form sold for about two hundred dollars a month. For some reason, this less expensive compound wasn't indicated for Lo's treatment. However, when I saw that we were charged $8,400 for a thirty-day course of the prescribed drug, I was shocked. The difference was so staggering, I placed some phone calls to check other sources' prices. Sure enough, a mistake had been made and the bill was twice the amount it should have been. The pharmaceutical supplier agreed to refund the insurance company for the difference. Don and I were as excited as the insurers that Lo's million-dollar cap — a savings account, if you will — was replenished as well.

I was just starting to fill out the appropriate claim forms after dinner one evening when Lo peeked around the corner, holding a ballpoint pen, a tablet and her school directory. "Mom, you know when we were in Dr. Kramer's waiting room yesterday and we saw those brochures about Great Strides?"

I had to think for a minute. "Great Strides. Mmmm . . . you mean the fundraising event for CF? The walk for a cure?"

"Yeah, the one they're going to have all over the United States on the same day."

"What about it?"

"I was thinking I could do that." Lo's smile was radiant. "Do you care if I call some people and ask them to help me?" She waved the directory enthusiastically.

"I think that's a terrific idea," I said. She had gone along with whatever we'd asked her to do regarding CF her entire life, but this was the first time she'd taken the initiative to act on her own.

She skipped back to her room and shut the door. A few minutes later, I could hear muffled laughter and talking. Two hours had passed when she rushed out to the living room where I was still working away.

"Guess what, Mom? I have four hundred and thirty dollars already! Isn't that awesome?"

"Are you serious?" I laughed, sharing her excitement. "That's incredible! What did you do — call the whole school?"

"No, but every single person I called wanted to give." No wonder, I thought, listening to the bubbly optimism in her voice. I knew that most people at Monte Cassino were aware that Lo had cystic fibrosis, but I had no idea how receptive they would be to her efforts.

The next few times Lo made calls I listened to her pitch. "Hello, Mrs. Miller, this is Lo Detrich. You know that disease I have . . . cystic fibrosis? Well, we are having an event to raise money for research. I'm going to walk six miles to help find a cure. Would you sponsor me?"

I thought about what my little girl was doing. How many children are willing to spend time and effort raising funds in the first place? And how many are willing to spend that time in between grueling hours of therapy and breathing treatments?

A few days later, she had another idea. "I want to have a bake sale to help raise more money for Great Strides. It'll be an advertisement for the event. I'll bake all the cookies and we can have the sale on Amma and Dido's driveway. Tons of kids walk by their house after school." Amma and Dido, being loving grandparents, were thrilled that Lo wanted to use their front yard for the sale. Lo baked dozens of cookies and brownies over the next several days. A classmate offered to come over and help. They decided to schedule the sale on a school holiday when Monte Cassino had parent-teacher conferences. We loaded up the car with the baked goods and headed over to my parents. We pulled out card-tables and chairs, my mom ironed picnic table-cloths and cut flowers from her garden for centerpieces — we hauled over Lo's cash register and made signs. Shortly before noon, the girls began to flag down passersby. During the lunch hour, nearly everyone from Don's office showed up in full support. When the public elementary school around the corner let out, the girls snagged dozens of kids on their way home. By late afternoon, nothing was left but a few crumbs for the birds.

We arrived at the Great Strides event, held at the Tulsa zoo, with boundless anticipation. There were about a hundred and fifty walkers, which was a super turnout for an event that was still considered new. The weather was warm and sunny, perfect for a stroll to admire the polar bears, sleepy lions, playful monkeys and synchronized swimmer seals. We weren't surprised at how much fun we had. But we were surprised at the announcement at the end of the walk. Our nine-year-old daughter had raised more money than anyone else — regardless of age — in Tulsa.

We hadn't even left the premises before she began scheming. "That was so much fun. I bet I can do a ton better next year. Maybe some of my friends would like to do it, too."

"Feel free to call us," several CF board members volunteered. "We'd love to be on your list."

On the way home, Don said, "I like your style, Lo. If you want to make something happen, you just gotta get in there and do it."

For the next several months, we centered our fundraising efforts on the chapter's other events, including the All Sports Ball. Our friends and relatives were still diligently supporting us through their contributions, attendance and participation. The All Sports Ball now consistently netted over one hundred thousand dollars a year, the Annual Golf Tournament was considered the best-run charity golf event in the area, and other events were attracting new faces to our ranks.

Lo frequently posed for publicity pictures and continued to attend almost every event. But her enthusiasm for the walk enabled us to see the potential for this event's growth. "When are the brochures going to come out for Great Strides?" she asked one wintry day.

"Since the event's not until May, I don't think they're running late just yet," I teased. "Are you already thinking about it?"

"I'm ready to start making phone calls, Mom."

"That's terrific. Maybe you could get an early start by writing a letter this year. You could go through our address book and pull out names of people we send Christmas cards to."

"I like that idea," Lo said.

"You get the letter ready and I'll make copies and address them."

The next month, Jo Ann Winn, the executive director at the CF office, invited Lo to come and call members of the board from there. "We'll give you an office to use," she said — magic words to our entrepreneurial-minded daughter. Jan Jackson, the special event coordinator gathered appropriate phone numbers for Lo to call. Lo didn't hesitate to call anyone she suggested. She loved getting to turn her love for playing business into real life experience. She spent several afternoons after school at the CF office calling board members and local businessmen. By the day of the second annual Great Strides event, Lo had increased her previous year's record ten times by collecting more than six thousand dollars. Again, she was the chapter's top fundraiser.

As an incentive to walkers, the national CF Foundation offered prizes for achieving various levels of collections. As any child would be, Lo was enthused about the possibility of winning prizes. But in addition to the television she earned for herself, she was allowed to pick another prize. "I think Amma and Dido need to have a cordless telephone. They practically have to run through three rooms to get to their old one. If they were sick and needed to call for help, they couldn't do it. I'm going to give them a phone for their fiftieth anniversary."

How like Lo to think of someone beside herself. It was this spirit of love and giving that made everyone involved with Lo want to work all the harder to erase cystic fibrosis from her life.

Chapter 37

ANGELS IN
WAITING

*O*ur attitudes were constantly lifted
by the thoughtfulness of angelic
friends and relatives. Their actions
could provide role models for anyone who wants to help but
isn't sure what to do.

"Hi. How is she?" Cheryl Thomas called one morning, knowing Lo had been sick for several days.

"Not good," I replied. "Dr. Kramer just called. He wants to
admit her to the hospital." Years of admissions had come and
gone since our initial hospital experience. We had become veter-
ans of intravenous infusions at home, but sometimes Dr. Kramer
preferred to have Lo go to the hospital so he could monitor her
condition for a few days first. Nuclear x-rays and sophisticated
forms of pulmonary function tests were among those easier to
administer on an in-patient basis. Oftentimes culture reports
required antibiotics be used that had to be monitored for toxicity

problems as well.

"I'll be right over," Cheryl said. In times of crisis, it didn't matter what else was going on in her life, she acted as if there wasn't a place in the world she'd rather be. Don and I had known Cheryl since college. Her beauty, wit and grace seemed to magically diffuse tension. She applied a blend of charm and artistry that somehow made even the most difficult situations almost entertaining.

This particular morning, she appeared within the hour ready to accompany us to the hospital. Once we were taken to Lo's room, Cheryl leaped into action. "Well, let's see, Lo," she said, eyeing the usual whitewashed hospital wall. "We just can't live with this room looking so dreary and cramped. What we need is a little color here and there. Did you bring any stuffed animals with you?"

The beanie baby craze had just begun. "I have a few beanie babies," Lo said, rummaging through her backpack. "Would these help?" She lifted up two handfuls of colorful creatures.

"Perfect," Cheryl said. She took the stuffed toys and used them to appoint the stainless steel apparatus looming over Lo's bed. Surveying the room again, she said suddenly, "Tell you what. Why don't I go pick up some lunch and then we'll see what else we can do to perk up this room." We found out that afternoon what other items she intended to pick up when she placed a flower arrangement in the windowsill, colorful magazines on the table and provided Lo with a needlework project to while away the hours. Three days later on Saturday night, she and her son, Will, showed up with a Chinese feast, complete with tablecloth and chopsticks.

Cheryl's selfless generosity was combined with a gift for knowing how to go about helping. More often than not, she took care of our needs before we even realized what we were missing.

Phil Eller, Don's law partner, and his wife Mece, also took on the weight of additional responsibilities necessitated by our situation. Phil never hesitated to offer his time in handling business when crises demanded Don's absence from the firm. Mece provided untold hot meals on a moment's notice when illness precluded my cooking.

Sidney Selinger, a childless retiree, represented a contingent of faithful volunteers whose enthusiasm maintained the fundraising force on our behalf. Their efforts renewed our hopes that, in spite of our own circumstances, others would field the fight to find a cure.

Cathey Cravens, my niece, dedicated every spare hour she could for years before leaving for college. Her patience and willingness to be another set of eyes and ears for me allowed all of us to survive many crises as she ran errands, babysat, listened, and willingly assisted in any task I couldn't complete. In her absence, Monica Furr, also a niece, stepped in.

Another group of angelic helpers included the faculty and staff at Monte Cassino. Fortunately for us, St. John Hospital, our home away from home, was located only a block away from the school. During the same admission in which Cheryl acted as interior design specialist, a nurse peeked in one morning to say, "You all have some visitors. In fact, you have a lot of visitors."

We could hear hushed voices and the clatter of shoes in the hall. As the nurse stepped out of the way, the voices shouted, "Surprise!" In walked Lo's entire fifth grade homeroom class. Mary Fitzpatrick, her teacher, had organized the field trip. For the next hour, her classmates treated Lo as royalty. They covered the walls with posters and cards, climbed on the bed for a group photo and watched part of a movie on the pediatric portable VCR. Their visit provided a critical connection Lo needed to maintain her relationships with her schoolmates. The lasting

effects of the laughter and affection heard that morning undoubtedly accelerated her recovery process.

"Whenever you get to feeling a little better, I'll come over to
your house and help bring you up-to-date on what you've
missed," teachers offered. "Don't worry about your school work,
Lo. We know you try as hard as you can to keep up. We'll make
sure you learn what you need to know." Flexibility, compassion
and skill were the framework within which the school staff oper-
ated as guided along by Principal Pete Theban and Sister Mary
Clare.

Another welcome face to our world was that of Maureen
Beasley. She and Lo struck up a friendship at the end of fifth
grade that continues on. Her loyal support of Lo during hospital
visits won our hearts. Maureen and her family accepted Lo as
one of their own and Maureen became a regular visitor to our
house as well.

A chronically ill patient and the caregivers who must focus
their lives around her are constantly threatened by the potential
to become isolated from the world. The requirements of dealing
with the disease are constant. There is rarely a reserve of energy
left for initiating contact with others. Our friends worked to minimize our loneliness. The value of their calls, cards and visits can
never be underestimated. We only wished that life would somehow bring opportunities for us to respond in kind.

Family, too, was a source of invaluable support. Our parents
and siblings, their spouses and children, maintained a sincere
interest in our welfare, kept abreast of research studies and participated in fundraising events.

Since my mom and dad lived in Tulsa, they continued to keep
an open door to the girls for our occasional weekends away. And
when Lo was forced to miss school for extended periods of time,
she enjoyed the opportunity to spend the day at Amma and

Dido's as a change of pace.

It's typical for people to respond to an acute situation in which someone is hospitalized or ill. Efforts may help an individual over that one hump in their lives until they get well or weather the storm that is sure to blow over eventually. What was not typical in our case was the continuation of helping hands, year after year, again and again. People brought hot meals to the hospital or to our home, invited Jane to sleep over, sent flowers or mementos, or just called to say hi.

The staff at St. John's treated us as though we were part of their family. Their warmth and sincerity minimized what could have been a very perfunctory relationship. They recognized our experience with chronic illness gave us a distinct of expertise.

Chronic illness is constant. It doesn't go away. But even though we accepted it as part of the dynamics of our family, the demands it placed on us never grew any easier. Though in public we'd try to deny it, the fact is that we never 'got used' to the strain. Our friends, heroes one and all, silently acknowledged this and managed to step in at just the appropriate times, so we never bore the burden alone.

Chapter 38

STEADY AS
A ROCK

ashing dishes at the kitchen sink, I looked out the back window to see a familiar masked man deftly whirling a Weed-eater up one side of the fence and down the other. I surveyed the work he had already finished — the cleanly swept porch, the straight-edged borders of white cement and green grass, the piles of dead limbs tautly tied in orderly stacks. As if in rhythmic stride, he side-kicked a weather-beaten volleyball across the yard, which Lucy jubilantly retrieved. Having completed his sculpting, he slid the mask, dripping with sweat, over his head. Glancing up through the window, he caught me spying and waved.

Prompted slightly by guilt from the comfort of my air-conditioned vantage point, I quickly filled a huge plastic cup with ice water and ventured out the back door. "Hi, Big D. How about a cold drink?"

"Man, it's hot out here," Don accepted my offering and wiped his face with the already drenched t-shirt he'd pulled off. "That's it for me."

We walked around the yard together as Don gulped his water. "Needs a load of dirt," he decided, eyeing the occasional burrows and knolls, courtesy of Lucy and her explorations. "And I'd love to get rid of that trampoline. The girls don't use it any more."

"Yes, as a matter of fact they do," I defended the absentee jumpers. "Not as often as they used to, maybe, but I can't stand the thought of getting rid of it."

"It kills the grass underneath," Don insisted.

"So what?" We walked on in silence, then stopped under the massive oak tree whose branches almost spanned the width and depth of the back yard.

"Remember the Swiss Family Robinson swing set?" I laughed.

Don nodded, throwing the last of the unmelted ice cubes from his cup onto the ground. "Now that was unique. The girls sure spent some time on it, didn't they?"

"Lo was only four when you put it up," I reflected. "I was scared to death with you and Mark shinnying up that trunk like you were lumberjacks. You guys must have used a million feet of that yellow ski rope. But it was pretty and it was functional. Between the swings and the ropes, Lo and Jane and their friends had some great times. They just loved to climb up the ship's ladder and soar out on the line you hung on from that limb." I pointed upward, looking at the now bare branches. I once again saw little girls giggling and screaming with terrified delight as they dropped and swung from off the wooden landing Don had rigged up. "I miss those days."

"It goes too fast, doesn't it?" Don agreed, a twinge of

sentiment in his voice as well. His gaze shifted from the tree to Lucy as she nosed the volleyball hopefully toward his feet. "Wanna go for it, girl?" he obliged, once again sending the ball across the yard.

I looked at my husband, gathering up the last of his yard tools. There was still no hint of gray, even at his temples. The rich brown hair had been cut shorter through the years and was now being routinely buzzed by a long-standing barber. Don had never been one for styling. Years of consistent exercising had maintained his athletic physique. He easily grabbed up two heavily laden lawn bags, one in each hand, and wielded them through the gate around to the front.

Don Detrich. Strong, confident, steady. He hated to be called steady, I mused. He thought it was tantamount to being called boring. Nothing in the world could be further from the truth. What Don termed as boring, I cherished as dependable. Throughout the ordeal of having a child with chronic illness, he had been the one individual with whom I could share my greatest hopes and deepest fears.

I'd heard so many sad stories of other families destroyed by the consequences of cystic fibrosis. Patients whose parents had abandoned them or left them to other relatives to nurse. Parents who had died prematurely from heart attacks or other stress-related illnesses. Couples who had to work several jobs trying to make ends meet to pay for medicines, insurance, and other CF-related expenses, eventually splitting up out of exhaustion, frustration and burn-out.

Without a doubt my relationship with Don had been tested through the years. My will was strong and so was his. We both cherished our independence. Given a project, we generally approached it from opposite directions. Fortunately, most of the time, our differences provided a balance. But there had been *issues about which we vociferously disagreed.*

A few years ago, an acquaintance of ours came over to visit. After the girls had gone to bed, we started talking about relationships. Our friend told us that her marriage was in a state of turbulence. She and her husband couldn't seem to adequately communicate their needs to one another but didn't want their marriage to fail. Yet they had come to the point of complete frustration.

Don and I had also been struggling with one particular aspect of our relationship. It just seemed like no matter how hard one of us tried to explain his or her position, the other one couldn't understand. We'd both end up angry, bitter and resentful. As our friend described her predicament, I assumed Don was identifying with their frustrations as much as I was. But what he said opened up a barrier which had plagued our communication lines for years.

He explained that even though we, too, had areas of disagreement, the one thing he could count on was that we were committed to one another. Period. No matter what happened, we wouldn't bail out on the marriage or our love for one another. As I listened to him, I realized that much of the resentment and bitterness I felt when we'd disagreed was because of my own insecurity in our relationship. I realized that my insecurity was unfounded and was getting in the way of our marriage.

Sometime after this incident, I found myself reflecting on the impact of having a husband whose commitment was unconditional. I thought about the craziness our marriage had endured, from chronic illness to early morning intruders. With each crisis, Don and I had come together, drawing strength from our differences, seeking refuge in our moments of weakness.

"Big D, I need to talk to you," I found Don as he sat reading in his favorite chair.

"One sec, just let me finish this last page," he said, following the words with his finger. Setting the book down, he looked up at me. "Okay, I'm all ears."

I sat down on his lap, put my arms around his neck and leaned my head on his shoulder. There were no words that came to my mind. I realized I had no need to talk to this man I loved. As he encircled me in his arms, I closed my eyes and felt the warmth of his body. I listened to his breathing — even and sure. Twenty-some-odd years of living together, one day after another, with this same, steady man. I sighed with grateful satisfaction.

"What's the matter?" he asked.

"Not a thing," I answered, kissing his cheek. "Not a thing."

Chapter 39

THE HENRY ZARROW AWARD

*E*ight years had passed since the Henry Zarrow Award had been created. Eight recipients had been honored for their contributions to the Sooner Chapter of the Cystic Fibrosis Foundation, including our friends Kathleen and Markus Hilti, Bill Thomas, and Bob and Mary Stewart, who had also been there from the beginning with us. Terry and I had even won the Zarrow Award the year Lo was eight. Now she was thirteen, and as former recipients, Terry and I were part of the nomination committee for the 1997 honoree.

As usual, the committee met and initially reviewed the fact that the award was the highest honor an individual could attain for contributing to the success of the Sooner Chapter of the Cystic Fibrosis Foundation. It served as a reminder that our cause was one driven by need, by generosity and by love. Within this framework, we proceeded to identify the candidates who best fit the requirements.

"There's no question in my mind who should receive the award this year," one of the former honorees volunteered. "I nominate Lo Detrich."

For a single moment, there was a hush in the room. Terry and I were speechless. As we looked around, it was obvious that the other committee members were in total agreement with him.

"Why didn't I think of that," one said.

"She's the perfect choice," added another.

A minute later the vote was cast and Lo won by acclamation. It was true that Lo's fundraising efforts for cystic fibrosis had been unequalled. She frequently missed school and social activities to represent CF at area businesses, make speeches at local fundraising events and contribute in any other possible way. It was also true that she never complained her sacrifice was too great. She was always willing to help. It was this attitude, combined with her remarkable accomplishments with Great Strides that prompted the nomination committee to so enthusiastically endorse her as the 1997 Henry Zarrow Award winner. We were both proud and humbled.

A special recognition ceremony was planned in conjunction with the chapter's annual dinner. The whole affair was planned as a surprise to Lo. A local corporation sponsored the cost of inviting dozens of her loyal supporters and relatives. Beautifully printed invitations were sent requesting that no one let the surprise slip. The dinner was held at The Gilcrease Museum, a renowned gallery of Southwestern art. Attendees enjoyed a gourmet dinner followed by the annual review of the chapter's successes during the year. Throughout the evening, there was an atmosphere of excitement and anticipation.

The Zarrows were still actively involved in the support of the Sooner Chapter, although Anne had become seriously ill and 'Mr. Henry,' was temporarily disabled by a broken toe and recent surgery. Still, he insisted on attending the function, so he could personally recognize his friend Lo. He delivered the speech describing Lo's achievements, saving the announcement of her name till the end. Everyone in the room but Lo knew he was talking about her.

THE HENRY ZARROW AWARD SPEECH
(Delivered by Mr. Henry Zarrow, January 6, 1998)

Every now and then, our paths cross with someone whose impact on our lives is profound. Our honoree is just such an individual. Your presence here tonight evidences this fact.

Yes, we are bound by a common great cause. Each of us wants to participate in some way in the discovery of a cure for cystic fibrosis. All of us hope to alleviate the suffering that CF patients endure every day of their lives.

But cystic fibrosis in and of itself is just a word. It is not until we relate that word to a person that our mission holds meaning. It is not until we know someone with CF that we understand the ugliness, witness the pain, and can more appropriately share the burden that accompanies this devastating disease.

Our honoree's impact has provided us with a lesson, which motivates us far beyond sympathetic aid. She has taught us that where there is suffering — there is determination. She has shown us that where there is sadness — there is also room for joy. She has inspired us with her own tenacity and courage in hopes of an ultimate victory.

She has made us laugh through our tears. She has shown us that Faith abides, both when pain persists and when prayers are answered. Yet rather than sit back and wait for others to find a cure for cystic fibrosis, she has decided that she, too, will participate in the challenge. Emboldened by the support of family and friends, her efforts to fuel the fight against CF have been wildly successful.

And yet, in the spirit of those recognized by the Henry Zarrow Award, it has not been without great effort on her own part that this success has been achieved. She has made hundreds of phone calls, written countless letters, recruited workers, attended meetings, made presentations. And she has never lost appreciation for the generosity of those who willingly work with her — side-by-side.

Along the way, she has met and made friends with peers — of all ages. No one is too young or too old, has means too great or small, to join forces in the battle.

And yet, as you may have guessed by now, our honoree's battle is far more personal. Her efforts to find a treatment for CF have been sandwiched in between the demands of current therapies and ravages that the disease has already left on her.

Yes, it is in part because of the fact that we share a common goal and because we have witnessed the valiant struggle of this one individual that we so readily join forces with her. But it is also her ability to lead us lovingly, innocently, with hope and faith that has so profoundly impacted each of our lives and made it a privilege to recognize her tonight. Please join me in honoring our 1997 Henry Zarrow Award recipient, Lo Detrich.

The spontaneous standing ovation and the hug from Mr. Henry caught Lo completely off-guard. Her smile was dazzling, and her tears happy. Stepping to the podium, she beamed at everyone. She acknowledged how much she appreciated their presence and support which had helped her raise funds. "I don't know what to say except thank you all so much!"

Suddenly, from around the corner, a group of her classmates appeared. Mary Fitzpatrick, the same teacher who had led Lo's class to the hospital, had also been instrumental in encouraging the participation of Monte Cassino students in Great Strides. She had reserved the school bus in order to bring several of Lo's friends to and from the event.

As if that recognition weren't enough, we found out that a select group of friends had taken it upon themselves to spread the word about this little girl who had touched their hearts. Each had made a sizeable donation, which, when combined, amounted to fifty thousand dollars to the foundation in Lo's honor, as a recognition of her spirit in facing her disease.

What a tribute. What a testimony to the idea that life is meant to be cherished and lived fully, regardless of its challenges. This is a part of the spirit of Lo which inspired the title of this book. It is this spirit that she exhibits every day whether she is in the public eye or the privacy of our home.

The true test of the award came in the following months as Lo proceeded to carry on with Great Strides as usual. "It's fun," she said. "I look forward to it every year." It was the spring of 1998 and Lo took on her biggest job ever for CF. She became the chairman of the Tulsa Great Strides event. Lowell Faulkenberry, who had chaired the event for our chapter since its inception, came up to Terry and me at a reception. At the time he was also serving as chapter president. "I don't know why I didn't think of this before," Lowell shook his head. "Lo has been our top fundraiser for Great Strides every year. She's the major reason it has been such a success. What do you think about the idea of asking her to be the chairperson? I don't see any reason why it has to be an adult."

Needless to say, we were thrilled that our twelve-year-old had been recognized as such an integral element to the event. Knowing how determined she would be to see another year through, we agreed to let her be in charge. Lowell assured us that he would continue his effort as a back up in case Lo got sick.

Lo took the appointment seriously and set about organizing an army of helpers. She recruited several friends, mostly children from school, to serve on a committee. They began to meet after school at our house or the CF office. The staff provided Lo with her own room and desk again from which to direct her activities. She made appearances at local businesses to generate enthusiasm, wrote letters, made phone calls. The results broke all previous records. She had been responsible for generating over twenty thousand dollars, more donations than anyone else in our region, which includes several states, thereby qualifying for two free roundtrip tickets to any city in the continental U.S., courtesy of American Airlines. The entire Tulsa event garnered more than sixty thousand dollars, paving the way for the future.

The following year, Lo again chaired the event. About the time she was beginning her efforts, a board member sent her a personal letter. This woman was in charge of another event that would be held later in the year. Her goal for that event was fifty thousand dollars. In her letter, she challenged Lo to raise fifty thousand dollars as well. Lo did not hesitate to accept.

The numbers had grown so large, however, it became clear that time would not enable her to meet her goal without instituting some new fundraising methods. "What you need are some matching donors," Kathleen Hilti suggested. Lo thought the idea was brilliant, particularly since Kathleen and Markus were willing to participate as matching donors themselves.

During Lo's chairmanship of Great Strides, Terry and I ran into a friend who had attended a function with several other business leaders. "You know, we were all talking about Lo at the party," he said. "We felt honored when we got a call from her. We all agreed that it was a good thing she didn't realize she could have asked for anything. We'd have given it to her!"

By the day of the event, Lo had collected over fifty thousand dollars, and, combined with the rest of the walkers, over one hundred thousand dollars were turned in. A few weeks later, we were thrilled to find out that Lo had raised more money than any other young individual in the United States.

"You know, Lo, that without each one of these people being motivated to give so generously, you would not be raising all this money," I told her one night at bedtime.

"Yeah, it's pretty amazing, isn't it?"

"There's a lot of good causes out there, that's for sure."

"I'm glad they think CF is a good cause."

"Me, too. But I'm also glad that you appreciate you shouldn't get all the credit for the success of Great Strides."

"I think I know what you mean. We've got a lot of good friends who are just nice people. They are the ones who should really get the credit."

"You're pretty young to understand that, little girl. But that's exactly what I'm talking about."

"I'll try not to forget."

There was no flippant, "I know, Dad" — no arrogant attitude, no condescending comeback. Just quintessential Lo.

Chapter 40

A Sister's
Compassion

*A*s we watched our children grow
up, we often wondered what Jane
was learning from having a little
sister with chronic illness. Her ability to express herself from an
intellectual standpoint exceeded her age but her capacity to
explain her emotional state did not. In fact, when it came to
expressing her feelings about our situation, Jane typically withdrew into a tight-lipped silence.

We had heard that siblings of children with life-threatening
illnesses struggle with guilt resulting from ambivalent feelings of
jealousy, anger, bitterness and resentment mixed with love and
fear. These are described as children who are made to feel less
important than their ill sibling, because the disease constantly
demands the parents' full attention. In our family's case, the
attention Lo also received because of her fundraising activities
took even more attention away from Jane. It was easy to

understand why Jane felt neglected but clinical explanations such as this do not go far toward salving a young heart confused by tragedy. The why and wherefore of catastrophe continues to baffle the brightest minds among us.

It took years of living with her little sister, of watching what she had to do to fight cystic fibrosis, of witnessing her survive the endless series of infections — for Jane to allow Lo's challenges to share some footing with the pain she herself endured because of the situation. We had little idea how she felt until the middle of her senior year in high school. Jane had been applying to various universities and had to write a personal essay as part of several of the applications. We received our first inkling of the tremendous admiration Jane has for Lo when she allowed us to read one of the essays. There before us on the page was a touching insight into Jane's heart, feelings long protected by tear-stained silence.

"A Day in the Life"
by Jane Detrich

Beep, beep, beep. As I roll over to hit the snooze button, I notice the time. It's 5:45 in the morning. What?!? I never get up this early. As I begin to change the alarm, I hear a voice, "Here's your treatments, honey."

Excuse me, treatments? And then I listen to my own voice say, okay. Soon after, I feel the slimy plastic in my mouth. I smell something foul. I taste gross broccoli and asparagus and pepperoni all at once. I feel a cold mist entering my lungs; it makes me cough. Choke is a better word. After fifteen minutes of inhaling the mist and gagging, I am done. With that one, anyway.

I get out of bed and put a scratchy gray vest on my shoulders. I fasten three Velcro straps, place my foot on a lever and flip a switch. I begin to shake uncontrollably. Shake and cough. Cough and shake. The sound of a jet engine landing in my room forces me to turn up the music on my CD player full blast to be able to hear anything at all. By now, I am fully awake and realizing how much I wish I could be asleep again. Shake, shake, shake. Cough, cough, cough. I feel I am going to cough up a lung. I am trembling and coughing and have developed a headache. After a few minutes, I have to stick the slimy plastic back in my mouth and start on another different kind of disgusting smelling, foul-tasting treatment.

Ding. Thank heavens. The sound of that timer is the best sound I've ever heard. I'm done with the shaker — the air compressor, done with the breathing treatments. Finally, I can go about the business of getting ready for school like a normal kid — for a few minutes anyway.

I'm dressed and ready — I've got my books and assignments. I walk to the kitchen and sit at the breakfast table. I put a bite of oatmeal in my mouth and immediately hear my mother say, "Did you take your pills, yet?"

I look down. Sitting at my place are at least twenty pills — white, pink, blue, green, brown. How am I going to take them all again? They're huge! I ram them into my mouth. I feel my mouth full of milk and boulders. I swallow. I am relieved when they slide down my throat.

Now, I'm in the car going to school. I begin to take inhalers and nose sprays. One puff — I hold my breath until a cough interrupts. Another puff — another disgusting taste in my mouth. More coughing. We pull into the parking lot. At least at school I shouldn't have to do anything for hours.

WHATEVER! When the lunch bell rings, I walk straight to the nurse's office. She hands me inhalers — the same ones I took on the way to school. I open my lunch sack — just as many pills are sitting inside as there were at breakfast. This is crazy, I think.

Now, I'm at home again. It's 3:15 in the afternoon and time to take more breathing treatments. An hour later, I'm swallowing more pills so I can have a snack. Later at 7:00 o'clock we eat dinner. I'm taking more pills. I think again, this is crazy. I do my homework, call a friend, and then it's time for the morning scenario again — more slimy, smelly, nasty breathing treatments — more shaking from the inside out from the jet engine air compressor. It takes another hour and a half. I fall into bed at 10:00. I try and sleep but the sounds and smells of the day interrupt my dreams. So does the coughing. I hate this disease called cystic fibrosis.

Beep, beep, beep. I roll over and hit the snooze button. I notice the time — 7:15 a.m. It's today. Yesterday, I wasn't me. Yesterday, I was my sister. My sister? What! And then I realize, God allowed me to be my sister for one day so that I could experience what she goes through every day.

It's amazing. I can't believe it. I could never do it. She has no choice. No choice? I realize that through being my sister for only one day, I come to understand her better than I have in fourteen years of talking to her every, single day. By being my sister, I learn to appreciate her more. I learn to forgive her for doing little things that she's not supposed to do, or for not doing things she should — things that she does have a choice about and chooses not to do. Not clearing her place doesn't seem so significant anymore. Instead of yelling at her, it's more important that I take her dish and ask her if there's anything else I can do to help her. Can I be her friend?

In spite of the tastes, smells, time demands, I realize she somehow manages to be happy. I realize she is always smiling. She inspires people to look at the bright side of things and never give up no matter what the odds are. She doesn't feel sorry for herself either. She shares her joyful outlook with others every day. I think, in fact, that I am proud of my little sister. Even though she does things that make me mad, it's who she is that is so special. I realize her life makes the world a better place.

By being her for just one day, by seeing the world as she sees it, I appreciate that maybe things are not so fair for her either. When I am back in my own skin again, I see the world a little differently, a little more clearly. I see that for both of us, life is not so easy, but it is precious.

Chapter 41

THE BIG
PICTURE

∽

*U*nderneath the reality of day-to-day life in the Detrich household, was the awareness that we were running a race, a very real race against time and disease. Occasionally we would get news about the race, and how Lo was faring as the clock ticked incessantly.

This news was most objectively measured by pulmonary function tests — tests that measure the ability of the lungs to move air in and out. Inhaling adequate oxygen and exhaling the waste of carbon dioxide is the primary job of the lungs. The typical cystic fibrosis patient loses a few percentage points of lung function each year. The evidence that the lungs are gradually deteriorating becomes obvious as pulmonary function scores decline.

Periodically, Lo took PF tests at Dr. Kramer's office by blowing into a mouthpiece connected to a small computer which could then graph out the various elements of her breathing capacity and compare it to that expected of a healthy individual. Because the patient has to be able to breathe in and out consistently for the test to be considered accurate, a certain amount of maturity is necessary. Typically, pulmonary function tests aren't conducted until a patient is three or four years old.

When Lo first began taking PF tests, her scores approached the normal expectation for a child her size and age. But each year, the downward curve of the computer's graph told a bleak story. As the CF foundation accumulated its most accurate patient census including the history of each patient's disease process, we were able to compare her condition to that of other children her age with CF. When we did it became clear to us that Lo's challenges were immense.

Added to that dismal fact, Kathleen Hilti and Terry took a trip out to Phoenix, Arizona in the winter of 1999 and met with one of the researchers who had been credited with finding the CF gene in 1989. They wanted to get an update on the status of a cure. "He told us that there are many mysteries left to solve before we eradicate CF," Terry reported sadly. "I had thought once we found the gene, a cure was only a couple of years away. It's been ten years since then. We can hope for a cure. But it might not come in time to help Lo."

It was a bitter pill to swallow. We had entered into the world of fundraising as an antidote to the pain we felt as we watched our daughter suffer from an incurable disease. We were gratified that our efforts would someday benefit thousands of patients — and their families. But, the reality was that our motivations were also selfish. It was our daughter we most wanted to cure. It was our own fight against cystic fibrosis that gave us the incentive. The truth was that regardless of the breakthroughs in research, we were dealing with a disease that was still as deadly as it had been the day Lo was diagnosed.

I recalled the last time Lo had been hospitalized. The repeated episodes of pneumonia were taking away her ability to bounce back completely. Though she was now back at school, then she had been so weak she could hardly walk from her bed to the door. In an effort to bolster her spirits, I had taken her on marathon rides in a wheelchair, down the corridors, down the elevators and outside. I could still hear her laughter as we sped along the sidewalk. I could picture her smiling appreciatively up at me, saying, "This is so much fun, Daddy!"

Even after all these years, it was hard for me to admit my daughter's disease was an overwhelming foe. I couldn't release my desire to protect Lo, and Terry, and Jane from fear, heartache, sadness, and pain — even though I had learned I could not fight that battle alone. Not for my family — not even for myself.

As Lo approached her fifteenth birthday, our little family's efforts to face and conquer the evil villain called cystic fibrosis would be just that — a little family's effort. But I had learned something in the fifteen years of my child's illness that I didn't know at its onset. It was something that Lo had apparently known all along. She reminded me of it during a speech she delivered to her classmates in the spring of 1999.

She asked the principal of Monte Cassino if she could talk to the students during a school mass. She invited us to attend. In the days prior to the service, we encouraged her to practice her speech. "I know exactly what I'm going to say, Mom and Dad. You don't need to worry about it." Her air was confident. We were anxious to learn why.

On the day of the mass, Jane, Terry and I sat towards the back of the school chapel. The faculty was spread around the room. Lo's friends were on every row. She walked up to the microphone without a note. She looked out at the audience serenely and happily.

"Most of you know me," she said. "Most of you have been with me all of my school life. You've seen me take pills and medicines. In fact you've reminded me to take them when I've forgotten. You've made sure I ate my lunches so I'd stay healthier. You've heard me cough when I've been sick but you've never made me feel like you think I'm sickly. And when I've had to be absent for a long time, you've never forgotten me. You call me or come visit me so I don't have to be alone.

I know that I have a disease and that there is no cure for it. Yet. But you make me feel as if I am not fighting cystic fibrosis by myself. Every day, my family is there and my friends are there. Your support of me and your love for me is the best medicine I take.

When I work on raising funds for research you are there with me, raising them, too. You will be there with me at Great Strides making it fun for everyone. I don't know why I have cystic fibrosis or if there will ever be a cure for me. But I do know that if having this disease is why I have felt so much love from you and from my family, I would do it all over again just the same. Maybe God gave me this disease so I would understand how important loving and life is. Even when it seems that we don't understand our own worlds, He does. He is the one with the big picture."

Through tears of pride and joy, I smiled up at my little girl. I put one arm around my wife and the other around Jane, pulling them as close as I could — this precious little family of mine. In that moment, I knew our journey had not been just about a race for a cure. That would ultimately be only one facet of the road upon which we were traveling. The journey was about something even more powerful, something that would sustain us regardless of the outcome of the race. Life and all the experiences that make up its richness, the tandem of joy and sorrow, agony and ecstasy — love and the strength of its ties — faith in something that will ultimately make sense of what appears to be senseless, all these aspects of each day are what make the journey worth taking.

In that moment, I realized that this must have been the essence of the promise God made to Terry that night prior to Lo's diagnosis. Nearly fifteen years had passed since He had assured her He was going to take care of Lo forever. Lo's words evidenced to me that her spirit was infused with the power of His gift. And somehow I was learning that the gift He had given Lo was the same gift He had given to me.

Chapter 42

A MAY TO
REMEMBER

*I*n everyone's life there are events that mark major milestones. In May of 1999, so many milestones occurred that our family will forever cherish the entire month. First of all, both girls graduated — Jane from high school and Lo from middle school. Jane received her diploma with honors and was offered multiple scholarships from distinguished universities. She was grateful that both Don's parents and mine were able to attend and she looked forward to entering the next phase of her life, to testing the bounds of independence and adulthood.

In January, Lo was named a Prudential Spirit of Community Award winner for the state of Oklahoma. She was invited to attend a recognition ceremony in Washington, D. C., at the beginning of May in which the announcement of the national award winners would take place. Don and I decided we would *also attend the four-day event. It turned out to be a life-changing experience.*

The opportunity to meet one hundred young teens whose boundless enthusiasm and energy had prompted them to serve their communities in a variety of capacities gave us renewed hope that individuals really can make a difference. Whether it was to assist victims of abuse, poverty, disease, or violence or to help create opportunities for better education, the honorees' efforts inspired us.

"Mom and Dad, I can't believe I got to come to this," Lo said at one point. "These kids are amazing." Throughout the four days, she was able to develop friendships with peers who lived in all areas of the U. S. She listened to their stories and the wisdom of speakers such as Magic Johnson and Edward James Olamos. On Monday, we were all treated to lunch at the National Press Club to hear of the announcement of the ten national award winners. We went, fully convinced that each and every one of the hundred honorees were worthy of such recognition.

After lunch, the President of the National Association of Secondary School Principals, Dr. Curtis L. Voight, described the partnership between The Prudential's Initiative and that of NASSP. "We understand that children are our future and that each of these young adults exhibits the kind of character and leadership we need in the United States."

Mr. Art Ryan, the president of The Prudential, explained that a panel of esteemed judges had selected the ten finalists, each of whom would be awarded a $5,000 scholarship and named one of America's top ten youth volunteers. He then introduced Congressmen Byron Dorgan and Bill Frist, who proceeded to announce the winners. After six finalists had been named, Senator Dorgan said:

"*From Monte Cassino School in Tulsa, Oklahoma — Lauren Detrich. Lauren Detrich has struggled with cystic fibrosis all her life. But despite the heavy burden this disease has placed on her, she has been an energetic fundraiser for cystic fibrosis since the fourth grade. Two years ago, she was asked to serve as the Tulsa chair for the cystic fibrosis foundation's Great Strides Walk-a-Thon and she raised $20,000 for the event.*

Last year she again chaired the Tulsa Walk-a-Thon and set her fundraising goal even higher. Despite three hours of physical therapy and breathing treatments each and every day, Lauren made hundreds of phone calls, wrote reams of letters, spoke at numerous events and encouraged friends to join her efforts. And, by the end of the campaign, Lauren had personally raised an astounding $50,000, making her the nation's number one fundraiser. Says Lauren, "I want kids with cystic fibrosis to be able to wake up one morning and just go outside and play. I didn't have that chance."

Ladies and gentlemen, for courageously turning her own crisis into an effort to help others and for contributing significantly to the search for a cure for cystic fibrosis, and for being an outstanding role model, we are proud to present a Prudential Spirit of Community National Award to Lauren Detrich."

The audience whistled, cheered, and gave Lo thunderous applause. She was ecstatic. She walked up to the stage grinning from ear to ear, shaking the hands of the dignitaries and posing for pictures as the cameras flashed wildly. Then she approached the microphone to give her acceptance speech.

"*I'd like to thank Prudential and the NASSP for giving us this opportunity to be here and to bring kids together like this. It's showing people in our own community how cool it is to help other* people. When you help other people, it changes their lives. It's saved mine. People have gotten involved with me and raised money. I wasn't expected to live past twenty when I was little and now I'm expected to live past thirty.

But I also say you could die in a car wreck tomorrow. So instead of just living a miserable life and thinking of how bad things could get I just say I'm going to try and change that and I'm going to go and raise money and beat this and then we're all going to have a great life together.

And I would just like to say that you guys out there — you deserve this medal just as much as me. It doesn't matter how much you raise, it matters what you do. When you guys are out there helping people like this, you're changing a life. People want to be like you. And I want to be just like you all, too."

To be fourteen years old, to be recognized by others as having accomplished something extraordinary, to be able to speak in The National Press Club was an exhilarating experience for Lo and for us. We were again honored and humbled.

That afternoon, we went to the office of the national cystic fibrosis foundation. Though we had known Lo was going to be presented with another award there, we didn't know the details surrounding it. On the previous Friday night in Chicago, Frank Deford, who since his daughter Alex's death had served as chairman of the national foundation, emceed the annual meeting. There, in her absence, he presented Lo with the 1999 Outstanding Volunteer Leadership Award. A video of the presentation was played for us with the entire national staff giving Lo a resounding ovation.

When we returned to Tulsa, yet another honor was bestowed on our daughter. The Tulsa Chapter of the American Red Cross named her as an Everyday Hero. She had been nominated anonymously with other community heroes whose actions had earned them the distinction of recognition because they had saved lives, or made a significant difference in the community.

Finally, on the eve of her graduation from middle school, Lo received another award. Her classmates and the faculty of Monte Cassino elected her May Queen. It was the highest honor that could be given an eighth grade graduate. The May Queen was supposed to be that student whose actions and attitudes most closely resembled that of Mary, the mother of Jesus.

It was an extraordinary month filled with excitement and wonder. We were extremely proud of the manner in which Lo accepted her recognition as she acknowledged with humble appreciation all those who had supported her over the years. She knew it was their generosity that provided her the opportunity for such exceptional achievements. As Don and I revisited the memories of battling cystic fibrosis, of raising funds for a cure, and of the tremendous level of commitment we had made to our little family, we, too, couldn't help but feel a certain sense of victory over the catastrophe that had occurred one day in our lives in October of 1984.

THE ROAD AHEAD

Our memorable May could have been the ending of a magnificent story of triumph over tragedy. It was triumphant. And it did serve to prove that joy can be found regardless of tragic circumstances. Each and every day provides us with reminders of both the joy and the tragedy. Each and every day presents us with the challenge to embrace the minutes lived in between our beginning and ending. It is in this way that we can genuinely appreciate the amazing gift of life.

But ours is a true story. It cannot have the kind of ending found in fictional books or movies. We are still on the journey. And there is still a road ahead upon which we must travel.

APPENDIX I

We have come to appreciate that all of us are created equally. Not in the framework of a constitutionally protected right, but rather in the sense that nobody gets a free ride. Viewed over the spectrum of each individual's life, bumps in the road await all of us. They come in many shapes and sizes and at the most inopportune times. Some may be more visible than others but all are significant to those who endure them.

As a community and as individuals, strength is to be gained in the sharing of common experiences. To know that others have faced adversity and survived buoys the spirit. As we have shared our experience, we now invite you to share yours. Allow others in need to draw strength from what we hope will be a compilation of the "community of spirit" between those who have overcome adversity. Please send your story, address and day/nighttime phone number to:

Terry and Don Detrich
c/o Mind Matters, Inc.
P. O. Box 52503
Tulsa, Oklahoma 74152-0503
Email: www.SpiritofLo.com
Tollfree: 1-877-222-2095

We are all victors, not victims.
Together, we will make a difference.

APPENDIX II

If your child or someone you love has been diagnosed with cystic fibrosis, there are better resources than ever to help you deal with the myriad of questions you will undoubtedly have.

CYSTIC FIBROSIS FOUNDATION
6931 Arlington Road
Bethesda, Maryland 20814
www.cff.org
1-800-FIGHTCF

The primary source of information regarding the disease is the Cystic Fibrosis Foundation, located in Bethesda, Maryland. The CF Foundation's mission is to "assure the development of the means to cure and control cystic fibrosis and to improve the quality of life for those with the disease." (Source: www.cff.org Homepage)

Under the direction of the CF foundation are **local chapters,** which are involved with raising funds for research, and the **CF Care Centers,** which are involved with patient care.

> ✓ **Fundraising Events** - As we discovered, helping to raise funds for our daughter's disease provided us with hope and inspiration. For information regarding your nearest local chapter, contact the foundation.

> ✓ **Patient Care** - Over 110 CF Care Centers are located throughout the U.S. For information concerning these centers, contact the foundation. Addresses for these centers can also be found at the CFF web page.

✓ **Contributions** – If you would like to make a donation to cystic fibrosis research, your check can be made payable to the *Cystic Fibrosis Foundation,* and mailed to the address above. We would also encourage you to support the local events held in your area.

✓ **Questions** – Obviously, your patient's personal physician will be your primary source of information with regard to cystic fibrosis. However, there are other sources of information available that may help supplement your need to understand the disease and how you can best care for a patient. Several of these sources are listed below. Unless indicated, publication copies can be obtained by ordering through the foundation.

- *Commitment* – The national newsletter of the Cystic Fibrosis Foundation, *Commitment* is issued seasonally and can be requested from the foundation. Articles include latest research updates as well as results of chapter fundraising events.
- **CFF Web Page** – **www.CFF.org** – The foundation's web page is a major source of information regarding all facets of its activities.
- *Homeline* – Published by CF Services, Inc., a wholly-owned, for-profit subsidiary of the CF Foundation, *Homeline* is distributed as a part of the home health and pharmacy service. Articles include information on CF-related topics particularly helpful for patients and caregivers. CF Services, Inc., 6931 Arlington Road, Suite T-200, Bethesda, Maryland 20814; 1-800-541-4959.
- **Facts About Cystic Fibrosis** – A card describing the major symptoms and research status of cystic fibrosis distributed by the CF Foundation. Also available at chapter offices.
- **Insurance Information** – General descriptions of the different kinds of policies, both public and private, are given on the foundation's web page.
- **Diagnostic Testing** – A brief description of the standard diagnostic cystic fibrosis "sweat test" is available from the foundation. The test is painless, and if conducted by a professional trained in the technique, provides the most conclusive information needed to diagnose the disease.

✓ Other Resources for Information

- **American Biosystems**   1-800-426-4424
                                   www.thairapyvest.com

- **Boomer Esiason Foundation**   www.esiason.org

- **Genentech**   1-800-551-2231
                                   www.genentech.com

- **Ortho-McNeil Pharmaceutical** 1-908-218-6000
                                   www.cfcare.com

- **PathoGenesis Corporation**   1-847-583-5442
                                   www.pathogenesis.com

- **Pari-Neb**   1-800-327-8632
                                   www.pari.com

- **Ross/Abbott Laboratories**   1-800-551-5838
                                   www.abbott.com

- **Scandipharm**   1-800-950-8085
                                   www.solvay.com

- **Solvay Pharmaceuticals, Inc.** 1-800-354-0026
                                   www.solvay.com

- **Cystic Fibrosis
  Legal Information**   Hotline: 1-800-622-0385

APPENDIX III

Perhaps you or someone you love has been recently diagnosed with one of the following diseases or conditions. Here are some resources you can contact.

1. **American Cancer Society**
   1599 Clifton Road N.E.
   Atlanta, Georgia 30329
   1-800-227-2345
   www.cancer.org

2. **Juvenile Diabetes Association**
   120 Wall Street
   New York, New York 10005
   www.jdfcure.org
   1-800-JDFCURE

3. **American Diabetes Association**
   1701 North Beauregard Street
   Alexandria, Virginia 22311
   www.diabetes.org
   1-800-DIABETES

4. **American Heart Association**
   National Center
   7272 Greenville Avenue
   Dallas, Texas 75231
   www.americanheart.org
   1-800-AHA-USA-1

5. **American Lung Association**
   National Office: 1740 Broadway
   New York, New York 10019
   www.lungusa.com
   1-212-315-8700
   or call: 1-800-LUNG-USA (You
   will be connected to a local
   branch in your state)

6. **March of Dimes**
   1-888-modimes
   www.modimes.org or
   Center@modimes.org
   1275 Mamaroneck Avenue
   White Plains, NY 10605

7. **Muscular Dystrophy Association**
   3300 East Sunrise Drive
   Tucson, Arizona 85718
   1-520-529-2000
   1-800-572-1717
   www.mdausa.org

8. **National Down Syndrome Society**
   666 Broadway
   New York, New York 10012
   1-212-460-9330
   www.ndss.org

9. **American Academy of Allergy, Asthma and Immunology**
1-800-822-2762
www.AAAAI.org

10. **Sickle Cell Disease Association of America**
200 Corporate Pointe, Ste 495
Culver City, CA 90230-8727
1-800-421-8453
www.sicklecelldisease.org

11. **Arthritis Foundation & American Juvenile Arthritis Organization (AJAO)**
www.arthritis.org

12. **Center for the Study of Autism**
www.autism.org

13. **The Epilepsy Foundation**
4351 Garden City Drive
Landover, Maryland 20785
1-800-EFA-1000
www.efa.org

14. **United Cerebral Palsy Association**
www.ucpa.org

ABOUT THE AUTHORS

Don and Terry Detrich have been married for twenty-five years. They are the parents of two daughters, Jane and Lo. The Detrichs reside in Tulsa, Oklahoma.

Terry is a graduate of the University of Tulsa. She spent several years as a marketing representative with IBM. In her spare time, she provides marketing consulting services and is a freelance writer.

Don has practiced law since 1976, the last twenty years as a senior partner of Eller and Detrich. He has also served as an adjunct professor of law at the University of Tulsa and is a frequent volunteer speaker to students at local schools. Don is currently a member of the national Board of Trustees of the Cystic Fibrosis Foundation.

For information
on speaking engagements:

Call: 1-877-222-2095

Write: Mind Matters, Inc.
            P.O. Box 52503
            Tulsa, Oklahoma 74152-0503

E-mail: www.SpiritofLo.com

*To join the battle against cystic fibrosis,
please make your check payable to:*

Cystic Fibrosis Foundation
6931 Arlington Rd.
Bethesda, MD 20814

THE SPIRIT OF LO

An Ordinary Family's Extraordinary Journey

(Please Print Clearly)

Your Name: _____

Your Street Address: _____

Apartment or Suite Number: _____

City/State/Zip: _____

Phone: Area Code ( ) _____
(If ship to address differs from billing address, please attach a separate sheet)

Number of copies _____ x **$14.95** each $ _____
   Add **$1.19** per copy (Sales tax - OK residents only) $ _____
   Add Shipping and Handling fee $ _____
     $3.95 for 1st book
     $2.95 for each additional book
   TOTAL DUE: $ _____

▶ *If paying by check,* **make check payable to Mind Matters, Inc.**
  Send completed form and check to address below.

▶ *If paying by credit card,* send completed form to address below.
  ❑ Visa   ❑ Master Charge

_____   _____
Credit Card Number   Expiration Date (Mo/Yr)

_____
Name as shown on Credit Card

     Mail form to: **Mind Matters, Inc.**
                   P.O. Box 52503
                   Tulsa, Oklahoma 74152-0503

To order by phone, call toll-free: **1-877-222-2095**
To order by E-mail: *www.SpiritofLo.com*

Please call for volume discount